A GUIDE

THE LA

GOODS VL......

DRIVING TEST

AND LICENCE

A GUIDE TO
THE LARGE
GOODS VEHICLE
DRIVING TEST
AND LICENCE

DAVID P SOYE

**KOGAN
PAGE**

First published in 1976 by Kogan Page Ltd
Second edition 1978
Third edition 1981
Fourth edition 1984
Fifth edition 1986
Sixth edition 1987
Seventh edition 1988
Eighth edition 1989
Ninth edition 1991
Reprinted in 1992
Reprinted 1993
Reprinted 1994

Kogan Page Limited
120 Pentonville Road
London N1 9JN

British Library Cataloguing in Publication Data

A CIP record for this book is available from the British Library.

ISBN 0 7494 0173 7

Typeset by The Castlefield Press Ltd., Wellingborough,
Northants.
Printed in England by Clays Ltd, St Ives plc

Contents

Acknowledgements

Great care has been taken in the preparation of this ninth edition and I would like to say thank you to all those people and organisations who so kindly offered their help and assistance. They are: Manchester Training for their valuable contribution; the Controller of HMSO for its permission in reproducing the numerous road traffic signs and markings; the Department of Transport and all those trainees who have taken the LGV Driving Test and who shared their experiences with me. I am sure you will find the book helpful, informative and easy to read. Finally, may I wish all those who are preparing for, or about to take, the LGV driving test all the very best and good luck.

Foreword

The author's principal object has been to gather together, in one handy volume, salient features extracted from a number of official and semi-official pamphlets and booklets issued for the help and guidance of those who aim to pass a Large Goods Vehicle (LGV) driving test, and to supplement these features out of his own experience as a qualified LGV driving instructor.

The highest practical value will be achieved by using the book in conjunction with expert instruction, *for which there is no substitute.* Instructor and trainee alike will use the question-and-answer sections not only as a series of checklists, but also as a readymade and comprehensive source of essential information.

Quiet study of the relevant text and exercises will broaden and deepen the trainee's appreciation of his instructor's aims, and, coupled with intelligent application and practice under expert tuition, will go a long way towards ensuring success under test conditions.

This edition incorporates such changes as there have been in the LGV driving test and gives up-to-date information regarding the various test fees, medical fees and licence fees, test cancellation waiting days and other changes in the PCV Driving Test and Youth Training in transport.

Manchester Training has pioneered transport training long before the LGV driving test became a legal requirement. We believe we have the best driving instructors in the country and we are proud to be associated with the author of this work.

Roy Wilson
Chairman
Manchester Training

Sources of Qualified Instruction

National Vocational Qualification (NVQ) for Large Goods Vehicle (LGV) Driving Instructors

The contribution made by the Road Transport Industry Lead Body in the field of LGV driver training has been paramount over many years. Many of the registered instructors have probably been trained to national standards and the standards are continually being improved.

Many private and commercial organisations who undertake LGV driver-training employ qualified instructors and those seeking high-quality instruction are advised to look for such organisations, a list of which can be found in Appendix 1.

Group Training Associations specialise in this type of training and particulars of these Centres can also be found in Appendix 1.

The National Council for Vocational Qualifications (NCVQ) is the Accrediting Body for the national vocational qualification for Large Goods Vehicle (LGV) Driving Instruction at NVQ Level III.

LGV driving instructors who have successfully completed an intensive course of training will receive a National Vocational Qualification (NVQ) certificate. In addition, their names will be added to the Register of qualified LGV Driving Instructors. If a candidate is in any doubt as to their instructor's qualifications he should ask to see the instructor's NVQ Certificate.

Sources of Qualified Instruction

ROAD TRANSPORT INDUSTRY TRAINING BOARD

This certificate is awarded to

F P MCHALE

having achieved a

NATIONAL VOCATIONAL QUALIFICATION

in

HGV DRIVING INSTRUCTION	Level	III

The following units of competence have been achieved:

ROAD TRANSPORT INDUSTRY TRAINING BOARD MODULES:

1. PERSONAL DRIVING ABILITY

2. DEMONSTRATION DRIVING WITH COMMENTARY

3. PRACTICAL "IN-CAB" INSTRUCTIONAL ABILITY

4. "IN-CLASS" TEACHING ABILITY

5. ASSOCIATED KNOWLEDGE

****

Date of Expiry: 20 JUL 95

Date: 2 AUG 90   Certificate No.: 43502306

C.C. Hodgson *C. C. Hodgson*

Director of Training Research and Development
Road Transport Industry Training Board

The NCVQ Certificate for LGV driving instructors

Chapter 1
Unified Driving Licence – General – Large Goods Vehicle/Passenger Carrying Vehicle

A driving licence is required by any person who wishes to drive a motor vehicle anywhere in the United Kingdom and in any Member State of the European Community (EC).

A provisional licence, or a deemed provisional licence, must be applied for or obtained in order to take a motor vehicle on the road for the purpose of learning to drive and taking the regulation driving test.

In order to account for the varying degrees of skills required to drive the different types of vehicles, there are 15 categories of vehicles as defined in the Motor Vehicle Driving Licence Regulations 1990. Within these 15 there are *five* main categories, as follows:

Category
(A) will cover motorcycles;
(B) will cover motor cars;
(C) will cover large goods vehicles (rigid);
(D) will cover large passenger vehicles;
(E) will cover articulated vehicles and vehicles drawing a trailer.

The full 15 categories are as follows:

Category	*Entitlement*	*Additional Categories*
A	Motorcycle (with or without sidecar) but excluding vehicles in category K or P	

Note: a provisional licence holder may not carry a pillion passenger even if that person is a qualified driver.

B	Motor vehicle with a maximum authorised mass not exceeding 3.5 tonnes and not more than 8 seats in addition to the driver's seat, not included in any other category and including such a vehicle drawing a trailer not exceeding 750 kg authorised mass.	B + E, B1, C1, C1 + E, D1, D1 + E, F, K, L, N and P

11

Category	Entitlement	Additional Categories
B1	Motor tricycle with an unladen mass not exceeding 500 kg and with a maximum design speed exceeding 50 km per hour but excluding vehicles in categories K, L or P.	
C	Large goods vehicles maximum authorised mass more than 3.5 tonnes.	
C1	Goods vehicle exceeding 3.5 tonnes but not exceeding 7.5 tonnes maximum authorised mass including those drawing a trailer not exceeding 7.5 tonnes maximum authorised mass.	B, B + E, B1, C1 + E, D1 + E, F, K, L, N and P
D	Small passenger carrying vehicles (between 9 and 16 passenger seats); passenger carrying vehicles (more than 8 passenger seats but not longer than 5.5 metres); all large passenger carrying vehicles (more than 8 passenger seats and longer than 5.5 metres).	
D1	Passenger carrying vehicle (not used for hire or reward) with more than 8 but not more than 16 seats, in addition to the driver's seat, and including such vehicles drawing a trailer not exceeding 750 kg maximum authorised mass.	B, B + E, B1, C1, C1 + E, D1 + E, F, K, L, N and P.
B + E	Combination of a motor vehicle in category B and a trailer with a maximum authorised mass exceeding 750 kg.	
C1 + E	Combination of a motor vehicle in category C1 and a trailer with a maximum authorised mass exceeding 750 kg.	
D1 + E	Combination of a motor vehicle in category D1 and a trailer with a maximum authorised mass exceeding 750 kg.	
F	Agricultural tractor but excluding any vehicle included in category H.	K
G	Road Roller.	

H	Track laying vehicle steered by its tracks.	
K	Mowing machine or pedestrian controlled vehicle.	
L	Electric vehicle.	K
N	Vehicle exempted from duty under s.7(1) of the Vehicles (Excise) Act 1971.	
F	Moped.	

The Unified Driving Licensing System

As from 1 June 1990, the Unified Driving Licensing System was introduced replacing the British Driving Licensing System as previously administered by the Department of Transport.

As from the above date a single document driving licence was introduced showing the categories of vehicles which a licence holder is entitled to drive.

In April 1991 Large Goods Vehicles and Passenger Carrying Vehicles were brought in line with the unified single licence system. This means that the previous system of separate driving licences for Large Goods Vehicles and Passenger Carrying Vehicles has been phased out. The unified licence will display *all* driving licence entitlements including full and provisional entitlements for motor cars, Large Goods Vehicles and Passenger Carrying Vehicles.

Unified Driving Licence for Drivers of Large Goods Vehicles (LGV) and Passenger Carrying Vehicles (PCV)

The first stage of the unified driving licence system came into effect on 1 June 1990 when the categories of vehicles covering motor cars and other light vehicles were displayed on the driving licence.

The second stage of the system covers the *Vocational Licences* ie large goods vehicle driving licence (LGV) and public service vehicle driving licence (PCV), which came into effect on 1 April 1991. As from that date the terms heavy goods vehicle and public service vehicle were changed for licensing purposes to *large goods vehicle* (LGV) and *passenger carrying vehicle* (PCV).

The new system of putting vehicles into categories replaced the previous system of putting vehicles into groups and classes and the following information compares the old HGV Classes 1, 2 and 3 and the PSV Groups to the new LGV and PCV Categories.

New LGV/PCV Licence	*Old HGV/PSV Licence*
Category C Rigid goods vehicle over 7.5 tonnes gross vehicle weight	Group A ODL plus Class 2 or 3 HGV

Category D

Passenger carrying vehicle   Group A ODL plus PSV

Category E

Articulated Vehicle and   Group A ODL plus HGV
draw bar outfit   Class 1 (2/3)

The stipulation relating to vehicles with automatic transmission still applies. This means that if a driver holds a licence for a vehicle with automatic transmission only, he will not be entitled to drive a vehicle with a manual gearbox except in the case of the licence being used as a provisional.

Existing licences remain valid until their expiry date and do not need to be exchanged to benefit from any new entitlement. Existing licence holders will be allowed to drive a range of vehicles that correspond to the new categories. Also drivers whose vocational licences come up for renewal will get the new entitlement automatically.

Applying For a LGV Driving Licence

The system of unified driving licences requires an applicant to follow a more simplified route from a motor car provisional licence to a LGV Category E licence.

For example, an applicant may apply for a provisional licence in order to drive a motor car. Having successfully passed the motor car driving test he will send his provisional licence and pass certificate to the DVLA who will issue a full Category B licence.

In order to drive an LGV, the applicant will be required to apply to the DVLA and have the LGV provisional entitlement added to the unified driving licence.

Having successfully passed the LGV driving test, the applicant will have to send his full unified driving licence to the DVLA who will issue the unified driving licence with the relevant LGV category displayed.

Conditions affecting a provisional licence and licence application procedures can be found in the succeeding text. Subject to the particular category of licence being applied for, the applicant will need to conform to one of the following examples:

Example 1

To obtain a provisional LGV entitlement the applicant must send:

1. Full ordinary driving licence
2. LGV Licence Application Form
3. LGV Medical Report Form
4. LGV Provisional Licence Fee £21.00.

Example 2

Where an applicant has recently passed the LGV driving test and needs to have the relevant LGV category entitlement added to the unified licence the applicant must send:

1. LGV Licence Application Form
2. LGV Pass Certificate
3. Full Driving Licence (showing LGV provisional entitlement).

Completed application forms must be sent to the DVLA, Swansea.

Applying for an Ordinary Driving Licence

When applying for any driving licence, all applications should be sent to the Driver and Vehicle Licensing Agency (DVLA), Swansea.

An application form can be obtained from any Post Office and care should be taken in completing it to ensure that all the information given is correct. Failure to answer all the relevant questions will undoubtedly result in delay in obtaining a licence.

Provisional Licence

Only when a licence application form has been received and accepted by the DVLA at Swansea will the applicant be sent his provisional licence. The applicant will not be permitted to drive until such time as the licence is in his possession.

Deemed Provisional Licence

The term 'deemed provisional licence' refers to the holder of a full or provisional licence who wishes to drive vehicles not covered by the existing licence.

Disabilities

A full licence which authorises a person to drive an invalid carriage or restricts that person to a vehicle of special construction or design does not carry provisional entitlement to drive any other type of vehicle. If a disabled person wishes to learn to drive a vehicle of a type not covered by his full licence, he must first apply for the appropriate provisional entitlement to be added to his licence. Driving licences issued to some disabled drivers may indicate that the vehicle(s) they drive must have all controls fitted so that they may be correctly and conveniently operated despite their disabilities.

Disabled persons must be satisfied that if stopped by an authorised person, eg a police officer, they can demonstrate that they are complying with the terms of the licence.

Drivers of any age with disabilities may not be eligible for the 'until 70' licence but may instead be granted a licence for one, two or three years as appropriate in accordance with the disability. All licence holders are required by law to notify the DVLA at Swansea of the onset or worsening of any disability that is likely to interfere with the safe handling and driving of a motor vehicle. Failure to give such information can result in a fine of up to £100 (RTA 1988 Section 94). Temporary disabilities not expected to last more than three months are excepted.

Driving and Cardiac Pacemakers

People who have not previously been granted a licence because of their heart condition, but who have since been fitted with a cardiac pacemaker, may now be granted a driving licence provided other conditions are satisfied.

(a) That the person is unlikely to be a source of danger.
(b) That adequate arrangements have been made to receive regular medical supervision by a cardiologist (such supervision continuing throughout the period of the licence).
(c) That arrangements are being complied with.

'Until 70' Licence

Full driving licences will normally be valid until the holder's seventieth birthday, and may be renewed at three-yearly intervals thereafter subject to medical fitness.

Visitors to the UK – Driving Permit

Under international conventions, if you are a *bona fide* visitor to this country, you may use your national licence or International Driving Permit (except LGV) for 12 months from the time of your last entry into the country. Anyone who becomes resident here must, however, pass a test and qualify for a British licence. New residents may drive under their foreign licences for 12 months after taking up residence. If, after that time, they have not already passed a driving test in the UK, they must take out a provisional licence, comply with the conditions attached to that licence, and pass the driving test before they can be issued with a full British licence.

New residents with foreign licences are given priority in booking a driving test, as are certain other categories of driver. Persons coming from any EC country and certain other countries* are exempt from the above requirements and may exchange their original licence for a UK licence provided:

(a) the licence to be exchanged is current;
(b) there are no other reasons why it should not be exchanged; and
(c) the category of vehicle entitlement remains the same.

---

*Australia, Austria, Barbados, Republic of Cyprus, Finland, Gibraltar, Hong Kong, Japan, Kenya, Malta, New Zealand, Norway, Singapore, Sweden, Switzerland, Zimbabwe or the Territory of the British Virgin Islands.

The cost of an exchange licence is £17.00 and applicants should send completed application form (D1), which can be obtained from any General Post Office, to the DVLA, Swansea.

International Driving Permit

For vehicles to be driven in countries where a British domestic driving licence is not accepted, an International Driving Permit is required. This can be obtained from the Royal Automobile Club, PO Box 100, RAC House, Lansdowne Road, Croydon, Surrey, or through the Automobile Association, or the National Breakdown Recovery Service, fee £3.00.

Change of Name or Address

If you change your name or address, you should complete the section on the reverse of your licence and return the licence to the DVLA at Swansea. A replacement licence will be issued free of charge. You may continue to drive while you are waiting for the replacement licence to arrive provided the licence is still current and you have not been disqualified or debarred from driving in the meantime. Failure to notify the DVLA of change of address or name could result in a fine of £400.

Minimum Age Limits for Driving

No person under the age of sixteen is allowed to drive a motor vehicle on the road. The minimum ages for driving the various categories of vehicles are:

Moped	16 years
Motor scooter, motorcycle and 3-wheel car	17 years
Small passenger vehicle eg constructed or adopted to carry not more than 9 persons including the driver, or small goods vehicle eg constructed or adopted to carry or to haul goods and is not adapted to carry more than 9 persons including the driver and does not exceed 3.5 tonnes permissible maximum weight (including the weight of any trailer drawn)	17 years
Medium sized goods vehicle eg constructed or adopted to carry or to haul goods and is not adapted to carry more than 9 persons including the driver and exceeds 3.5 tonnes but not 7.5 tonnes permissible maximum weight (including the weight of any trailer drawn)	18 years
Ambulance service vehicle (operated by a Health Authority in England and Wales or, in Scotland, the Common Services Agency)	18 years

Other motor vehicles eg goods vehicles exceeding 7.5 tonnes permissible maximum weight (including the weight of any trailer drawn). Articulated vehicles — 21 years

Agricultural tractor, specially licensed as an agricultural tractor and not exceeding 2.45 m. in width — 16 years

Road roller, not exceeding 11,690 kg unladen weight — 17 years
exceeding 11,690 kg unladen weight — 21 years

These age limits do not apply to vehicles being driven under the orders of Her Majesty's Service.

Chapter 2

The LGV Driving Licence Entitlement

Qualifications Required in Order to Drive a LGV

In order to drive a large goods vehicle the licensing authority must be satisfied that the applicant is a fit and proper person to have such entitlement added to the driving licence.

To have such entitlement the driver must:

    (a) Hold a *full* unified driving licence for *Category B*. The licence must be current and free from any restrictions which would prevent the driver from driving a LGV;

    (b) be medically fit;

    (c) have a good record of driving conduct; and

    (d) unless applying for a provisional entitlement have passed the LGV driving test.

A *medical report form* (DTp 20003) can be obtained from any Area Traffic Office. This detailed medical report form *must* be signed by the applicant consenting to the medical adviser at the DVLA receiving the report from the applicant's doctor. The medical must be carried out by a registered practitioner and it is he who must complete and sign the DTp 20003 and certify the applicant fit/unfit to drive LGVs.

The certificate is valid for four months and is not available on the National Health. Doctors' fees for such an examination vary but are normally around £45.00. Applicants need to conform to the above when applying for a LGV driver's licence entitlement for the first time or have reached the age of 45, after which a medical certificate has to be provided at five-yearly intervals.

On medical examination, evidence of any heart disorder, or an addiction to the consumption of alcohol or drugs may/will result in the GP signing the applicant unfit to carry out the duties of a LGV driver. The loss of any limb or physical disabilities will receive special attention, as well as the condition of arms, legs, hands and joints. Any mental ailment that could interfere with the duties of a LGV driver may also result in medical failure. Persons who are epileptic may not be eligible for the granting of a LGV driver's licence. During the course of the examination, the applicant will be subjected to a strictly controlled eyesight test, where he will be required to read letters from the test card.

A hand test will be included in the examination to determine the applicant's field of vision. Should the results of this test prove to be unsatisfactory the applicant may be rejected by the DVLA as being unfit to carry out the duties of a LGV driver, although applicants wearing contact lenses will no longer be rejected.

If there is any doubt as to the applicant's medical fitness to drive LGVs, the DVLA may require a further medical examination before deciding whether to issue a LGV driver's licence entitlement. In the event of a candidate failing a medical examination and then being refused a licence by the DVLA, an appeal may only be lodged upon the production of new medical evidence. Applicants with minocular vision will not be granted LGV driving licence entitlements.

Good record of driving conduct When deciding whether or not to grant a LGV driver's licence, the DVLA will take into account any driving convictions within the last four years. In the case of offences involving drink or drugs, the period is 11 years. Each licence application will be considered individually and will be judged on its own merit. The types of offence that will be taken into account are motoring offences, drivers' hours and records offences, and offences relating to the road worthiness or loading of vehicles. Particular attention will now be paid to driving licences with four or more penalty points. This will be subject to further consideration by the Traffic Commissioners as to whether or not an applicant is a suitable person to hold a vocational licence.

Conditions Applying to a Licence with Provisional Entitlement

When a candidate is about to learn how to drive and take a vehicle on the road in order to prepare for the regulation driving test, the holder of the provisional licence must ensure that the following points are complied with:

1. The provisional licence holder may drive the vehicle only when accompanied by, and under the supervision of, a qualified driver who has held a full current licence to drive that category of vehicle for at least three years. (Currently this does not apply to LGVs.)
2. The supervisory driver (driving instructor) must be at least 21 years of age.
3. The vehicle must display the prescribed 'L' plates, as illustrated on page 23, clearly to the front and rear of the vehicle.
4. A candidate preparing for a motor car test (Category B) must not drive on motorways; a candidate preparing for a LGV or PCV driving test may drive on motorways.
5. A candidate preparing for a motor car test (Category B) must not drive the vehicle when towing another vehicle or a trailer; this does not apply to a candidate who is preparing for a LGV driving test.

Renewal of a Unified Driving Licence

Under normal circumstances a unified driving licence will not come up for renewal until the holder's seventieth birthday although a licence holder with LGV entitlement will be required to renew his LGV entitlement at the age of 45 years and at five-yearly intervals thereafter.

When your licence is due for renewal, the DVLA will normally send you a computer-produced application form before your licence runs out. For this reason it is important that you keep the DVLA advised of any changes to your name and/or your address. If you do not get a reminder from the DVLA, you should use form D1 to apply for your new licence. You must allow at least three weeks for the new licence to arrive. Do not wait until the old licence runs out.

Note: On each renewal occasion the LGV licence entitlement holder will have to conform to the medical examination requirements.

Withdrawal of a Unified Driving Licence

Where a licence holder has been disqualified from driving, irrespective of what category of motor vehicle he was driving at the time of the offence, or, is refused a licence or has had his licence revoked, he is not allowed to drive any category of motor vehicle on the public road.

After the period of disqualification has elapsed the licensing authority will return the licence provided that:

1. The licence has NOT elapsed during the period of suspension.
2. The licence has not been revoked for any reason.
3. The period of suspension is no longer in force.

After the term of disqualification has elapsed the licensing authority may require the licence holder to pass a further driving test before reinstating the licence.

Withdrawal of an LGV Entitlement

The licensing authority at the DVLA retain the right to cancel or revoke the LGV entitlement from a driver's unified licence without court action if, in their opinion, the holder has shown himself to be unfit medically or otherwise to hold such entitlement, in which case the driver may appeal against the decision by:

1. writing direct to the Licensing Authority, asking them to reconsider their decision; or
2. appealing to a Magistrates' Court (England, Wales) or a Sheriff's Office (Scotland).

In the case of a candidate being refused a licence on medical grounds, only *new* medical evidence will be considered in an appeal.

Removal of a Disqualification

If a disqualification is imposed on a driver's licence the driver can apply to have the disqualification removed:

1. after two years, if the disqualification is for less than four years, or
2. after half of the disqualification period has elapsed, if it is for more than four years but less than ten years, or
3. after five years, if the disqualification is for more than ten years.

Should such an appeal fail, a period of three months must elapse before another application can be made.

Production of a Licence

If required to do so, a licence must be produced for examination by a police officer either on demand or within seven days at a specified police station.

Cost and Duration of a Unified Driving Licence

Full unified licence	£17.00	Valid until holder's seventieth birthday
Provisional Licence (not Category A) that can be changed for a full licence after passing the relevant driving test	£17.00	Valid until holder's seventieth birthday
Exchange Licence	£5.00	
Duplicate Licence	£5.00	
Category A Licence	£5.00	
Provisional Category A Licence	£5.00	Valid for two years

Note: A fee of £5.00 is made to a person who requires a new licence to be issued after certain disqualifications. In the case of drinking and driving offences the fee is £20.00.

Cost of Driving Tests

The fee for a standard driving test is £23.50. The fee for a LGV driving test is £55.00.

If an applicant needs to cancel a driving test appointment, five clear working days' notice must be given.

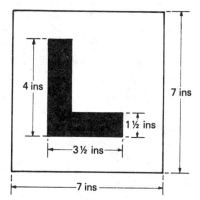

Prescribed Ordinary Plate

The prescribed 'L' plate required to be displayed on a vehicle for the purpose of learning to drive.

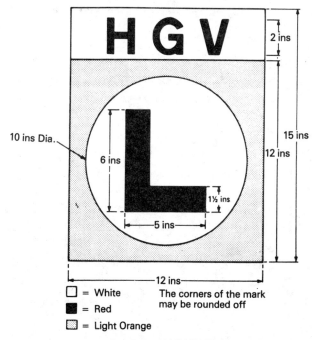

☐ = White
■ = Red
▨ = Light Orange

The corners of the mark may be rounded off

Prescribed HGV 'L' Plate

The prescribed HGV 'L' plate displayed on the LGV for the purpose of learning to drive. This plate will be phased out by April 1996. As from that date there will be no requirement to display. The prescribed ordinary 'L' plate will have dual purpose for all vehicles including Large Goods Vehicles, Passenger Carrying Vehicles and motor cars.

23

LGV Driving Test and Licence

At the time of writing, the following forms are currently in use although the format of the forms may change in due course.

Medical Examination

on an applicant for Large Goods Vehicle or
Passenger Carrying Vehicle driving entitlement

DTp 20003
Rev. Aug 91

• *Notes for the applicant*

If you knowingly give false information in this examination you are liable to prosecution.

Before you can be issued with entitlement to drive a LGV or PCV, the Secretary of State must be satisfied that you are fit for this type of driving. For this reason, your Doctor must fill in Part B of this Medical Report. You should then send it with your application to the Vocational Team, DVLC, Swansea, SA99 1BR. Failure to do so will delay the processing of your application.

Your Doctor will **not** be able to give you this report free under the National Health - you may have to pay a fee (this fee will **not** be paid by the DVLA). If you have any doubts about your fitness, consult your Doctor **before** you go for an examination. This form together with the application form must be received at DVLC within 4 months of the date of the doctor's signature.

Please fill in **Part A** of this form, make sure that you answer all the questions. Please write in CAPITALS.

☞ **Do not sign the authorisation at 9 until you are with the Doctor who is going to fill in Part B of the Report.**

• *Important*

By law, you must tell the Drivers Medical Branch, DVLC Swansea, SA99 1TU at once if you have any serious illness or disability which could affect your driving. This includes mental as well as physical conditions.

Part A To be filled in by the applicant	*Please answer all the questions and write in CAPITALS*

Date of first licence issue

| If you have held a HGV/PSV licence before, when was your first licence issued? | HGV | |
| | PSV | |

1. Full name

Date of Birth

2. Address

Home telephone number

Postcode

Work telephone number

Give the name and address of the doctor (or group practice) that you have been registered with for the last 12 months:

3. Name(s)

Address

Postcode

CLE861

Page1

An member's agency
THE DEPARTMENT OF TRANSPORT

24

● Notes for the Doctor

Please read these notes before undertaking the examination

Please complete Part B of this report, having regard to the 'Notes for Guidance' (1991 edition) published by the British Medical Association for Doctors conducting these examinations and where necessary, to the booklet 'Medical Aspects of Fitness to Drive' (1985 edition) published by the Medical Commission for Accident Prevention.

If you have any doubt about the applicant's fitness for this type of driving, please contact The Medical Advisory Branch, DVLC, Swansea, SA99 1TU.

Please tick the answer that applies and complete all answers.

The purpose of the report is to determine the applicant's fitness to drive LGVs or PCVs and it must be submitted with the application for entitlement to drive these vehicles. Failure to do so will delay the processing of this application.

The Medical Advisory Branch may need to make further enquiries if there is any doubt as to the applicant's fitness.

Applicants who may be asymptomatic at the time of completion of this report and obtain LGV or PCV entitlement, who later show symptoms of a medical condition should be advised to inform the Medical Advisory Branch.

The medical standards for LGV and PCV entitlement are higher than they are for ordinary driving entitlement. These standards are briefly explained below.

By Law a licence may not be issued if the applicant:-

- has had an epileptic attack since reaching the age of 5; **or**
- has visual acuity worse than 6/9 in the better eye or worse than 6/12 in the other eye or if corrective lenses are worn, has an uncorrected acuity in either eye of less than 3/60 unless he/she held a valid licence on 1.1.83 and still held such a licence on 1.4.91 when a lower standard will apply; **or**
- is a new monocular driver unless he/she held a valid licence on 1.4.91 and the Traffic Commissioner who issued the licence had knowledge of the condition before 1.1.91 and he/she has a visual acuity of not less than 6/9 in the remaining eye (or 6/12 if he/she was issued with a licence before 1.1.83); **or**
- is an insulin dependent diabetic, unless he/she held a valid licence on 1.4.91 and the Traffic Commissioner who issued that licence had knowledge of the condition before 1.1.91.

In addition the licence will be refused if the applicant:-

- has had a myocardial infarction, CABG or coronary angioplasty
- suffers persistent arrhythmia
- has uncontrolled established hypertension
- has had a stroke, TIA, or unexplained loss of consciousness
- has had severe head injury with continuing after-effects, or major brain surgery
- has Parkinson's disease, multiple sclerosis or Meniere's disease
- is being treated for or has suffered a psychotic illness in past 5 years
- has had alcohol or drug addiction problems in past 5 years
- has serious difficulty communicating by telephone
- has diplopia or visual field defect
- has any other condition which would cause problems for LGV or PCV driving.

● Important

Please do not write any comments or notes on this medical report form. Their inclusion could delay computer processing of an application. Any essential, additional information should be given in a separate letter and attached.

Part B Medical Examination - to be completed by the Doctor

Please give patient's weight [＿＿＿＿] (kg/st) and height [＿＿＿＿] (ft/cms)

Give details of smoking habits, if any [＿＿＿＿＿＿＿＿＿＿＿＿＿＿＿＿]

What is his/her alcohol consumption? [＿＿＿＿＿＿＿＿＿＿＿＿＿＿＿＿]

Please answer all questions

Section 1 Vision

Note: Visual acuities must be measured by Snellen chart (using spectacles or contact lenses if required).
If in doubt, please refer to local optician for assessment.
The applicant must meet 6/9 or better in one eye and 6/12 or better in the other (See NOTES p2).

		Yes	No
a	Does he/she fail to meet this standard?	☐	☐

i. If **'Yes'**, please state the acuities without lenses: ii. Acuities corrected by lenses:

Left: [＿＿] Right: [＿＿] Left: [＿＿] Right: [＿＿]

| b | Is the uncorrected visual acuity in either eye worse than 3/60 (equivalent to reading 6/60 line at 3 metres) without the use of spectacles or contact lenses? | ☐ | ☐ |
| c | Is the applicant without sight in one eye? | ☐ | ☐ |

Please give date when he/she became monocular [＿＿＿＿]

| d | Is there diplopia or evidence of a pathological field defect - eg hemianopia or quadrantanopia? | ☐ | ☐ |

Section 2 Nervous System

		Yes	No
a	Has there been an epileptic attack since attaining the age of 5 years?	☐	☐
b	Does the applicant suffer from epilepsy?	☐	☐
c	Is there a history of an episode or episodes of unexplained altered consciousness?	☐	☐
d	Is there a history of stroke, TIA, or vertebrobasilar insufficiency?	☐	☐
e	Is there a history of recurring Meniere's disease?	☐	☐
f	Is there evidence of multiple sclerosis?	☐	☐
g	Is there evidence of Parkinson's Disease?	☐	☐
h	Is there a history of major brain surgery?	☐	☐
I	Is there history of serious head injury with evidence of an intra-cerebral haematoma or compound depressed skull fracture?	☐	☐
j	Is there serious difficulty preventing adequate communication by telephone?	☐	☐
k	Is there a history of unexplained syncope or disabling vertigo?	☐	☐

Section 3 Diabetes Mellitus

		Yes	No
a	Does the applicant have diabetes mellitus? If **'Yes'**, please answer the following questions. If **'No'** proceed to Section 4.	☐	☐
b	Is the diabetes managed by:-		
	i. insulin?	☐	☐
	ii. oral hypoglycaemic agents and diet?	☐	☐
	iii. diet only?	☐	☐
c	Is the control of the diabetes unsatisfactory?	☐	☐
d	Is there evidence of:-		
	i. loss of peripheral visual field?	☐	☐
	ii. severe peripheral neuropathy?	☐	☐
	iii. significant impairment of limb function or joint position sense?	☐	☐
	iv. episodes of hypoglycaemia?	☐	☐

Section 4 Psychiatric Illness

		Yes	No
a	Has the applicant suffered or required treatment for a psychotic illness in the past 5 years ?	☐	☐
b	Has the applicant required treatment for a mental disorder with psychotropic medication within the past 6 months?	☐	☐
c	Is there confirmed evidence of dementia?	☐	☐
d	Is there a history of alcohol misuse in the last 5 years?	☐	☐
e	Is there a history of drug or substance misuse in the last 5 years?	☐	☐

Section 5 Musculoskeletal System

		Yes	No
a	Has the applicant a significant disability of the spine which is likely to interfere with the efficient discharge of his/her duties as a vocational driver?	☐	☐
b	Has the applicant any deformity, loss of limbs or parts of limbs, or physical disability (with special attention paid to the condition of the arms, legs, hands and joints) which is likely to interfere with the efficient discharge of his/her duties as a vocational driver?	☐	☐

Section 6 Malignant Growths

		Yes	No
a	Is there a history of malignant brain lesion, either primary or secondary?	☐	☐
b	Is there a history of bronchogenic carcinoma?	☐	☐

Section 7 Other Conditions

	Yes	No
Does the applicant suffer from any significant medical disability not mentioned above, which is likely to interfere with the efficient discharge of his/her duties as a driver?	☐	☐

Section 8 Cardiac

a Coronary artery disease

Is there a history of, or evidence of: **Yes No**

  i. Myocardial infarction? ☐ ☐

     (if 'Yes' please give date(s)) _____

  ii. Coronary artery by-pass graft (CABG)? ☐ ☐

     (if 'Yes' please give date(s)) _____

  iii. Coronary angioplasty? ☐ ☐

     (if 'Yes' please give date(s)) _____

  iv. Confirmed angina, whether or not treated symptomatically? ☐ ☐

b Cardiac arrhythmia and heart block

  i. Is there a history of persisting cardiac arrhythmia? ☐ ☐

  ii. Is there history of paroxysmal cardiac arrhythmia, in past six months? ☐ ☐

  iii. Has an ECG been undertaken? ☐ ☐

     If **Yes**, what abnormality has been shown? _____

  iv. Has a pacemaker been inserted? ☐ ☐

c Peripheral arterial disease

  i. Is there a history of aortic aneurysm, thoracic or abdominal, whether or not it has been repaired? ☐ ☐

  ii. Is there or has there been symptomatic peripheral arterial disease, with or without surgical intervention? ☐ ☐

d Blood pressure

  i. Is the established blood pressure (to the nearest 5 mm Mercury) 200/110 or over? ☐ ☐

  ii. Is medication required? ☐ ☐

     If **Yes**, does it cause giddiness, fainting, lack of alertness or fatigue? ☐ ☐

e Valvular heart disease

  i. Is there evidence of valvular heart disease, with or without heart valve replacement? ☐ ☐

  ii. Is the applicant taking anti-coagulants for the valvular heart condition? ☐ ☐

f Other cardiac conditions

  i. Is there a history of dilated cardiomegaly or hypertrophic cardiomyopathy? ☐ ☐

  ii. Has an X-Ray been undertaken? ☐ ☐

     If **Yes**, does it show significant enlargement of the heart, CTR> ·55? ☐ ☐

  iii. Has heart, or heart/lung transplant, or cardiac surgery other than CABG or aortic aneurysm repair been undertaken? ☐ ☐

  iv. Is there a history of congenital heart condition, whether or not treated surgically? ☐ ☐

Section 9 For Applicant

- *You must sign this declaration when you are with the Doctor who will be filling in Part B of this report*

I authorise my Doctor and Specialists to release confidential information to the Department of Transport's Medical Adviser if any matter affecting my fitness to drive arises:

- in connection with my application for my LGV or PCV licence;

- during the period that a licence (if granted) is in force; or

- in connection with my ordinary licence entitlement.

Applicant's signature:

Date:

Section 10 For Medical Practitioner

Signature of the Registered Medical Practitioner

Date

Name (in CAPITALS)

Address

Postcode

Telephone
(including STD Code)

Application for Large Goods Vehicle (LGV) or Passenger Carrying Vehicle (PCV) Entitlement

D2

Driver and Vehicle Licensing Agency

1. The notes on the attached sheet will help you answer the questions on this form.
2. You may also wish to read the information leaflet D200 available from DVLC, Vehicle Registration Offices (VROs) and Traffic Area Offices (TAOs).
3. Please write clearly in **BLACK INK** and **CAPITAL LETTERS** and ensure that all questions are answered and the form and any cheques are signed.
4. You **MUST** hold full motor car entitlement before you can apply for entitlement to drive larger vehicles.
5. The terms HGV and PSV are now referred to as LGV and PCV.

1. Your Details

Surname | Other names | Title (Please tick the box that applies to you): Mr, Mrs, Miss, Ms, Other (such as Dr., Rev.) please specify below | Are you: Male / Female

Address (see note A) | Postcode (Your licence may be delayed if the postcode is not quoted)

What is your date of birth? Day / Month / Year
What is your town of birth?
Daytime telephone number (if any)

2. To be answered by holders of LGV/PCV Licences issued in GB

Please tick appropriate box. Was your last licence: Full (LGV/PCV) / Provisional (LGV/PCV)

Are you enclosing your last licence? Answer Yes or No (All licences MUST by law be surrendered. Failure to enclose ALL licences may delay your application).

If NO, was your last licence: surrendered on disqualification, lost, destroyed, stolen, defaced or withdrawn for medical reasons? (Please indicate in box) Day/Month/Year

Expiry date on last licence (if known)

Driver Number from ordinary driving licence (if known)

Also make a note of your Driver Number at Section E on notes page

Are you applying as a member of the Armed Forces? Answer Yes or No
Are you a member of the Young Drivers' Training Scheme? Answer Yes or No

Name and address on licence if different from that written at box 1: Surname / Other names / Address / Postcode

3. What entitlement(s) are you applying for?

Please tick appropriate box(es)
1. Provisional entitlement to drive LGV / PCV / Both
2. Full entitlement to drive a LGV (category C)
3. Full entitlement to drive a LGV (category C+E)
4. Full entitlement to drive a PCV (category D)
5. Full entitlement to drive a PCV (category D+E)
6. Full entitlement to drive a PCV with up to 17 seats used for hire or reward (category D limited to 16 passenger seats)
7. Duplicate (because your licence has been lost, stolen, destroyed or defaced) (see note B)
8. Changes to your existing GB licence (see note B)
9. GB licence in exchange for your Northern Ireland or European Community licence
10. A new licence after disqualification
11. Exchanging your TAO licence for a new style licence

4. When do you want your entitlement to begin?

Day / Month / Year

Applications should not be made more than 3 months before entitlement is to begin. Licences cannot be backdated.

- If you are applying for your first provisional vocational entitlement, you must **NOT DRIVE** until you get the licence.
- If you have just passed your driving test, please send your test pass certificate with this form as soon as possible and write the category here
- Date of test | Serial No.
- Name of test centre
- If you already hold a licence to drive heavy goods or public service vehicles (HGVs or PSVs) see note B.

● Now turn over

5. Your Health *(see note C)*

YOU MUST answer every question in this section. If you do not, your application will be returned to you.
A medical report on DTp20003 (available from TAOs, VROs and DVLC) must be submitted with your first application for LGV or PCV entitlement and with every renewal after the age of 45. If you have submitted a DTp20003 within the last 12 months for an LGV/PCV licence you do not need to submit one now. A report must not be dated more than 4 months before the licence is to start. By law you may not be granted a licence if you have suffered or suffer from any of the conditions mentioned at note C.

Have you now or have you ever had any of the following?:-
(Please give details)

Liability to sudden attacks of disabling giddiness, fainting or blackouts	YES ☐	NO ☐	Date _____
Any heart condition, e.g. heart operation or pacemaker fitted	YES ☐	NO ☐	Date _____
Loss of sight in either eye, cataract, double vision	YES ☐	NO ☐	Date _____
An epileptic attack or epilepsy	YES ☐	NO ☐	Date _____
A stroke, head operation or head injury	YES ☐	NO ☐	Date _____
Alcohol or drug or substance continued misuse or dependency within the past 5 years (Do NOT answer YES for any drink driving offences committed)	YES ☐	NO ☐	Date _____
Any disability affecting arms or legs, e.g. Parkinson's Disease or Multiple Sclerosis	YES ☐	NO ☐	Date _____
Diabetes	YES ☐	NO ☐	Date _____
Any mental or nervous disorder requiring regular treatment	YES ☐	NO ☐	Date _____

If you have any other medical condition which could affect your driving, please give particulars here:

_____

_____

6. Details of convictions

In the space provided below, please give details of any court sentences or fixed penalties imposed.
If the space is insufficient, please give details on a separate sheet of paper and attach it to this application form.

For LGV and PCV driving licence applicants
Driving Convictions
- for offences relating to drivers' hours or records, or road worthiness or loading of vehicles for which you were fined or imprisoned in the last 4 years (2½ years if you were under 17 years of age at the time of conviction)
- for which you have been imprisoned for a period of more than 2½ years

For PCV driving licence applicants
You should also declare any sentence of imprisonment
- of more than 2½ years at any time or between 6 and 30 months in the past 10 years
- up to 6 months in the last 7 years or any fine or community service order in the last 5 years

Date of Conviction	Court (do not complete for fixed penalty offences)	Offence	Sentence or fine for fixed penalty offence (including period of disqualification, if any)
(a)			
(b)			

7. Declaration WARNING: If you or anyone else knowingly gives false information to help you obtain a licence, you and they are liable to prosecution.

Official Use Only

- **I apply** for a driving licence   *Delete if not applicable
- **I enclose** my current   ☐ * ordinary driving licence

  ☐ * vocational licences *(if applicable)*

  ☐ * EC licence *(if applicable)* see note B

  ☐ * Test Pass Certificate *(if applicable)*

  ☐ * Completed Medical Report form DTp20003 *(if necessary ~ see section 5)*

- **I enclose** the fee of   £ _____   Cheque/Postal Order No. _____
  (see note D)

- NB. Failure to enclose all relevant documents will delay the issuing of your driving licence.

- **I declare** that I have checked the details I have given and to the best of my knowledge they are correct and I am entitled to the licence for which I apply.

Sign here		Date	

- Now read notes E and F

Some notes to help you fill in this form

☞ *Keep this page – the notes will help you if you need to contact DVLC*

Please read the following notes carefully. They are about the arrangements for LGV/PCV licensing.

If you need any more information read leaflet D200. You can get this from any Traffic Area Office, Vehicle Registration Office or DVLC.

A Address

You must give your permanent address in England, Scotland or Wales.

B What entitlement are you applying for?

Provisional Licence

Provisional category C or D entitlement allows you to drive large goods or passenger carrying vehicles with a view to passing a driving test.

If this is your first application for provisional category C or D entitlement you must **NOT** drive until you get the licence. Normally this takes at least three weeks, but if you have a medical condition or a poor conduct record it may take longer.

When you have passed your test you should apply for a full licence within 2 years, otherwise you will lose your entitlement to drive vehicles covered by your test pass certificate.

Full Licence

If you are renewing your licence or you have passed a test you may continue to drive while your application is at DVLC. If you have held a licence to drive Heavy Goods or Public Service Vehicles (HGV or PSV) since 1 April 1986, you are not disqualified and are in good health, then you may drive as soon as your application has been received at DVLC. If you have a medical condition you are urged to seek advice from your doctor about whether or not you should drive.

Duplicate
To replace lost, stolen, destroyed or defaced licence

If you held an old style HGV or PSV licence you can apply to the TAO; **or** you can apply to DVLC if a new style licence incorporating your LGV/PCV is required. Applications should be sent to the address in section E.

If you are a holder of a new style licence also showing LGV/PCV entitlement you should apply on form D1 (obtainable at most post offices).

Exchange

For a driver

- who holds a current full GB licence and wants new categories added to it;

- who holds an old style PSV/HGV licence issued by a Traffic Area Office and wishes to exchange for a new style licence;

- who wishes to remove suspension details

  (All licences to be merged must be enclosed)

European Community Licence holders

If you hold a valid full licence issued in Northern Ireland, you can drive on your licence until it expires.

If you hold a valid full licence issued within the European Community you may drive on your current licence for 12 months. During this period you must apply for exchange of your EC licence. You should obtain a form D1 from a post office and send your application to DVLC, Swansea SA99 1AD.

If you are enclosing a European Community licence which gives cover to drive LGVs or PCVs and you wish that cover to be transferred to a British licence you will need to make your application on form D1 obtainable from post offices and on the attached form D2. **These forms must be returned together.**

Non EC Licence holders

Non EC foreign LGV/PCV entitlements (including Channel Islands and Isle of Man) are not exchangeable.
Please telephone the Driver Enquiry Unit on 0792 - 772151 for advice before submitting an application.

C Some notes about health

Please consult your doctor if you are in any doubt whether you should declare a medical condition.

1. Epileptic attacks – you cannot hold vocational entitlement if you have had an epileptic attack since you reached the age of 5, but this is currently under review.

2. Visual acuity (eyesight) – the eyesight standards have changed:

a. If you held a vocational licence on 1 January 1983 and still held such a licence on 1 April 1991 - you cannot hold vocational entitlement if your visual acuity is worse than 6/12 in the better eye **and** worse than 6/36 in the other eye **and**, if corrective lenses are worn, your uncorrected eyesight is worse than 3/60 in each eye;

b. If you held a vocational licence on 1 March 1992 – you cannot hold vocational entitlement if your visual acuity is worse than 6/9 in the better eye **and** worse than 6/12 in the other eye **and**, if corrective lenses are worn, your uncorrected eyesight is worse than 3/60 in each eye;

c. for all other cases – you cannot hold vocational entitlement if your visual acuity is worse than 6/9 in the better eye **or** worse than 6/12 in the other eye **or**, if corrective lenses are worn to meet these standards, your uncorrected eyesight is worse than 3/60 in each eye;

d. If you are a monocular driver - you cannot hold vocational entitlement unless you held a valid licence on 1 April 1991 and the Traffic Commissioner in whose area you reside or who issued the licence had knowledge of the condition before 1 January 1991 and you have a visual acuity in the eye of no worse than 6/9 (or 6/12 if you held a vocational licence on 1 January 1983).

3. Insulin treated diabetes – you cannot hold vocational entitlement if you are an insulin treated diabetic unless you held a vocational licence on 1 April 1991 and the Traffic Commissioner in whose area you reside or who issued the licence had knowledge of the condition before 1 January 1991.

D Payment Chart

Provisional entitlement	£21
First Full entitlement	FREE
Renewal	£21
Duplicate	£6
Exchange	£6
Issue of new entitlement after period of disqualification has ended	£12 (Full) £21 (Provisional)

When more than one entitlement is applied for, only the higher fee will be payable.

How to pay

● Please do not send cash or banknotes as the Department cannot be held responsible for missing remittances.

● Cheques or postal orders should be made payable to 'Department of Transport' and crossed 'Motor Tax Account'.

● Post-dated cheques cannot be accepted.

● Cheques drawn on banks outside the UK are not accepted.

● Please write your name, date of birth (or Driver Number if known) and address on the back of any cheques or postal order.

E Where to send your application   IMPORTANT correct use of the postcode will ensure speedier service

All LGV/PCV applications	VOCATIONAL SECTION DVLC, SWANSEA SA99 1BR	Provisional Applicants should write: "LGV/PCV FIRST APPLICATION" at the top of the envelope

Are you sending:

● Your last licence(s)? If so, write the driver number shown on your ordinary licence here

● Your test pass certificate? If so, write the serial number here   Date of test

● A medical report form DTp20003? (If applicable)

● A fee? If you are sending a fee make a note of how much you send or write FREE   £

If you send a postal order or cheque, write the number here   Make a note of the date you send the form to DVLC

F What you need to know after you have applied for a Driving Licence

● Always allow for time in the post to and from DVLC when you have sent your application. Please allow at least 3 weeks from date of posting (longer, if medical or conduct enquiries are involved) for your licence to arrive. If you do not receive it by then, please contact the **Driver Enquiry Unit, DVLC, Swansea SA6 7JL, or telephone 0792 - 772151** quoting your Driver Number and/or your full names and date of birth. (A call queuing system is in operation. If a ringing tone is obtained, please wait for an answer as calls are taken in turn).

● Please note if you have enquiries on vehicle licensing or registration then you should contact the **Vehicle Enquiry Unit. Telephone 0792 - 772134.**

● For **minicom users only** all enquiries should be directed to 0792 - 782756.

Driving without a licence
The law allows you to drive even if you do not actually have a licence provided:

● YOU have held a licence before and are still entitled to obtain one (that is you are not disqualified or the licence would not be or has not been refused on medical grounds); **and**

● A valid application for a licence has been received at the Driver and Vehicle Licensing Centre; **and**

● YOU can meet any conditions which apply when using that licence, such as those conditions which attach to provisional licence holders; **and**

● YOU do not drive without actually holding a licence for more than one year from the date of receipt of your application by DVLC.

Keep this page – the notes you have made will help you if you need to contact DVLC. If you need more information, read leaflet D200. You can get this from any Traffic Area Office, Vehicle Registration Office or DVLC.

An executive agency of
THE DEPARTMENT OF TRANSPORT

Printed in the UK for HMSO. Dd. WAB45 6/92 C1000 38369

Chapter 3
Penalty Points Endorsements

Where a driver has been convicted of any endorsable offence irrespective of what category of vehicle he was driving at the time of the offence, but has *not* been disqualified from driving, he will incur penalty points on the unified driving licence.

Each endorsable offence will appear showing the:

- date of the offence
- the offence code – ie exceeding the statutory speed limit on an ordinary road = SP 30
- any fine that may have been imposed
- the number of penalty points that have been imposed.

Note: Any disqualification periods will also be recorded on the new unified driving licence.

Each individual offence carries a specific number of penalty points and any driver who accumulates 12 penalty points within 3 years is likely to be disqualified from driving.

Penalty points range from one to ten. The maximum number is incurred for the most serious category of offences, ie reckless driving or offences related to drink and driving.

Courts have discretion to award a variable number of points for some categories depending on the seriousness of the offence.

The following penalty points chart indicates the number of points awarded against the description of the various offences.

Offence	Penalty points
Exceeding the national speed limit	3
Failing to stop at a school crossing	3
Using a special road contrary to regulations	3
Contravention of the pedestrian crossing regulations	3

Offence	Penalty points
Contravention of an order relating to street playgrounds	2
Causing death by reckless driving	*
Reckless driving	**
Careless driving	3–9
Driving or attempting to drive when unfit through drink or drugs	*
Being in charge of a vehicle when unfit to drive through drink or drugs	10
Driving or attempting to drive with excess alcohol in the body	10
Failing to provide a specimen for a breath test	4
Failing to provide a specimen for an analysis test	**
Racing on public roadways	*
Leaving vehicle in dangerous position	3
Failing to comply with traffic directions	3
Failing to comply with traffic signs	3
Contravention of the construction and use regulations	3
Driving without a licence	2
Driving with defective eyesight	2
Failing to comply with the conditions attached to a provisional licence	2
Driving while disqualified – under age	2
Driving while disqualified – by Court Order	6
Driving a vehicle without insurance	6–8
Failing to stop after an accident	8–10
Taking a vehicle without consent/driving or allowing oneself to be carried in it	8
Manslaughter or in Scotland culpable homicide	*
Stealing or attempting to steal a motor car	8
Going equipped to steal a motor car	8

* 4 penalty points if exceptional circumstances exist and a disqualification is not imposed.

** 4–10 penalty points depending on the particular circumstances if a disqualification is not imposed.

Where a driver has been convicted for two or more offences committed on the same occasion, the Courts will treat this as a single offence and the maximum number of points will be imposed on the licence. For example, if a driver is convicted for failing to comply with a traffic sign (three points) and using a vehicle without insurance (eight points), the higher number of points will be imposed on the licence.

Where a total number of penalty points has been exceeded within the three-year cycle, the licence holder will be disqualified for the following periods:

1. a minimum of six months;
2. a minimum of one year if previously disqualified in the three years before the latest offence;
3. a minimum of two years if previously disqualified more than once in those three years.

The court cannot reduce that minimum period or drop the penalty altogether because the offence was not serious in the circumstances, or because it will cause you hardship. Any hardship must be exceptional. A court might exercise its discretion if you would lose your job. You have a right of appeal either against conviction or disqualification to the Crown Court.

If you are convicted of driving with excess alcohol in the blood, you will still be disqualified for at least 12 months.

Where a driver is convicted of any of the listed offences, endorsements are usually automatic and compulsory unless there are special reasons. The courts have discretionary powers in these matters and may or may not endorse or disqualify as the case may be. Where a court has disqualified a driver, the court may order that driver to undertake a further driving test prior to the re-issuing of the licence.

Removal of Endorsements

Endorsements may be removed from a driving licence after four years from the date of offence, except for reckless driving which is four years from the date of conviction, and application should be made to the DVLA, Swansea, on form D1 (available from post offices).

Endorsements for drink offences and other driving offences remain on the licence for 11 years.

Dangerous and Aggressive Driving

The most recent proposals from the Department of Transport is an initiative to remove dangerous and aggressive drivers from the roads.

The proposals are aimed at those drivers who have a tendency of making their own rules when driving, often at the risk of endangering or inconveniencing other road users, particularly on motorways.

Aggressive and inconsiderate manoeuvres such as:

- driving dangerously close to the vehicle in front, particularly on motorways at high speed;
- cutting across lanes when leaving or joining motorways;
- passing vehicles on their near-side and weaving between vehicles at high speed.

These are only a few examples which describe *dangerous and aggressive* manoeuvres which do not conform to safe driving practice and do not reflect the actions of a safe and considerate driver.

The Penalties

Where a driver has been identified and convicted of dangerous and aggressive driving he/she will find the penalties very severe.

The proposed penalties will include a driving ban of up to five years after which the driver will be required to apply for a provisional licence and display the resulting 'L' plates until such time as he/she passes a new *extended driving test*.

Drivers with a drink and driving offence related to the above may also be required to attend a course of alcohol rehabilitation.

Details of these proposals will be made available in due course.

Chapter 4

The Large Goods Vehicle (LGV) Driving Test

The Department of Transport must be satisfied that those who wish to drive LGVs can do so safely and competently and be able to demonstrate that ability in the presence of a qualified LGV driving examiner during an official LGV driving test.

Candidates will be tested in both on and off the road situations.

Since the inception of the LGV driving test there has been very little change in the standard required, although there have been certain changes in the test procedures. The most recent change in the LGV test has been the revision of certain test routes which will eliminate high mileage and reduce duration time. The test has been reduced to 90 minutes.

Certain exercises have been reduced or removed altogether, the gear exercise has been modified, and is covered in greater detail later in this chapter.

Application for Driving Test

When making an application for a driving test, be sure to apply in good time, but do not ask for a test unless you are sure your driving is good enough to pass it. There is no sense in wasting your time or the examiner's and delaying tests for candidates who really are ready.

An application form for a LGV driving test can be obtained from a Traffic Area Office.

Every year hundreds of these forms are returned because they have been incorrectly completed; give *all* the particulars asked for on the application form, otherwise it will be returned and inevitably your test appointment will be delayed.

A common mistake is made in specifying the overall length of the vehicle. Applicants are required to take the OVERALL MEASUREMENTS. This means measuring from the extreme front of the vehicle, including any towing hitch which may be attached to the bumper or superstructure of the vehicle, to the extreme rear of the vehicle – which may also include such ancillary equipment as the chute of a concrete mixer or hose reels for tanker discharge. Often a mistake where the applicant has not included the examples given will

DRIVING STANDARDS AGENCY

Application for a Large Goods Vehicle (LGV) or Passenger Carrying Vehicle (PCV) Driving Test Appointment

For Official Use Only

DD	MM	YY	FTA	DD	MM	YY	FTA	DD	MM	YY	FTA	Accounts Use Only

Time	Time	Time	
Card	Card	Card	

Please read the notes overleaf before completing this form.

Ordinary Driving Licence Details

Driver No

Type of Licence (please tick one box)   Provisional [ ]   Full [ ]

Vocational Licence Held (please tick)

LGV [ ]   Provisional [ ]   Full [ ]

PCV [ ]   Provisional [ ]   Full [ ]

Expiry Date

Categories held

Personal Details

Surname

First name and initial(s)

Address

Postcode

☎ Home   Work

Disabilities and Special Circumstances

Details of Test Appointment

Choice of Centre

Unacceptable Days (tick any days you are unavailable)	Mon		Tue		Wed		Thur		Fri		Sat	
	am	pm	am	pm	am	pm	am	pm	am	pm	am	pm

Unacceptable Dates (enter details)

Earliest Date you will be available for test	Day	Month	Year

DLV 26

Test Vehicle Details

(please tick category)

Large Goods Vehicles		Man	Auto
Goods vehicles over 7.5 tonnes	C		
Articulated goods vehicles over 7.5 tonnes	C+E		
Goods vehicle and trailer combination of at least 15 tonnes gross	C+E		

Cab Seating Capacity

Overall Dimentions (metres)

Length   Height   Width

Passenger Vehicles		Man	Auto
All vehicles 8 passenger seats or more, **less** than 8.5 metres in length	D (limited to 16 passenger seats)		
All vehicles 8 passenger seats or more, 8.5 metres or **more** in length.	D		
All vehicles 8 passenger seats or more, 8.5 metres or more in length (with trailer over 1250 kg gross).	D+E		

Important: See notes overleaf

Fee enclosed   £

Cheque/postal order No

Signed

Date

Please fill in this box so that your appointment card can be sent to you.

Name

Address

Postcode

40

only be realised on the manoeuvring area when the applicant is taking the test.

At present the test fee is £55.50 and cheques or postal orders should be crossed and made payable to 'The Department of Transport' or the appropriate traffic area. Send the completed application form with the test fee to the Clerk of the Traffic Area in which you wish to be tested. You will find a list of LGV driving test centres and the addresses of the appropriate Traffic Area Offices on the application form. Send your completed application at least 28 days before the day you wish to be tested.

Test Appointment

When the application form has been received and accepted by the Department you will be sent a card which will tell you the date, time and place of your test appointment. This card also acts as a receipt for the test fee. If you need to cancel your appointment, five clear days' notice must be given exclusive of Saturday, Sunday and public holidays. For example, if your test appointment is for a Wednesday and you do not want to lose your test fee, you must inform the Traffic Area Office not later than the previous Wednesday that you wish to cancel the test, the five clear days being Wednesday, Thursday, Friday, Monday, Tuesday.

If you fail to keep your appointment, you will lose the test fee. If your test is postponed by the Department for any reason, another appointment (mutually convenient) will be arranged and the test fee will not be forfeited.

The Test Day

On the day of your test, make sure that you leave yourself enough time for the journey to the test station and just as important, enough time to check over your vehicle thoroughly (do not forget spare bulbs).

You will require your driving licence showing LGV entitlement and your appointment card. The driving test *will not* be terminated, nor will the candidate lose his test fee, if he cannot produce his licence at the time. However, at the end of the test the driving examiner will require from a successful candidate his driver's licence number and his present postal address. As you can see, it is in your own interest to carry your licence with you on test day.

Your vehicle must be suitable for the test and it must also be unladen. It should be clean and well presented both inside and outside. The windows and wing mirrors must be clean and there should be no loose articles in the cab likely to fall about during the test. The driving examiner may refuse to travel in the vehicle and consequently refuse to conduct the driving test if the vehicle is too dirty or if there is an excessive amount of equipment around the floor area and passenger seat and the examiner may define the vehicle unsuitable for test and the candidate will lose his driving test fee.

When presenting yourself for the test you must comply with the following requirements:

(a) The vehicle has been checked thoroughly and has enough fuel for the duration of the test.

(b) Stop-lights and indicators are clean and in working order. Your test could be terminated and test fee forfeited if your brake-lights are faulty. Driving examiners will allow a little time for a minor repair such as this.

(c) You must display 'L' plates on the front and rear of the vehicle.

(d) There is ample time for the test to be completed without exceeding your legally permitted hours of work.

Tests are arranged to a strict timetable and you must be at the test centre not later than the time shown on your appointment card.

Reception

On arrival at the test centre, park your vehicle in the area provided and report to the Reception. There is usually a room or an area where candidates can wait until the driving examiner appears. The examiner will ask the candidate to sign his test sheet, then to lead the way to the vehicle.

Reversing Exercise

The first part of the driving test will be the reversing exercise. This part of the driving test will take place on a special manoeuvring area within the confines of the test centre.

The driving examiner will normally accompany the driver to the vehicle and give clear directions as to how the driver should approach the manoeuvring area and where he should position his vehicle prior to the actual manoeuvre taking place.

This exercise will begin when the vehicle is in position at the bottom right hand corner of the manoeuvring area whereupon the driving examiner will give clear instructions as to how the exercise is to be carried out (see Figure 4.1 on page 44). Great care must be taken when doing this exercise as there is very little margin for error. The driver who tends to over-steer or under-steer or fails to position the vehicle *correctly* or tends to reverse too fast or erratically, will undoubtedly bring pressure upon himself. The driver must position the vehicle correctly, use the accelerator, clutch and steering effectively, and maintain a slow but constant speed, particularly with articulated vehicles.

Ideally the candidate should be able to position the vehicle correctly and complete the exercise without having to stop or without having to take a shunt. If a driver is unable to do this, he should not be taking the test as he is clearly not ready.

Braking Exercise

The second part of the driving test is the vehicle controlled stop or braking exercise. Here the candidate will be directed to another part of the manoeuvring area where this exercise can be carried out safely. The candidate will be directed to the start line/position where he will be required to park his vehicle in order to allow the driving examiner to climb into the vehicle. Only when the examiner is settled in and has secured all his paperwork will he give clear instructions as to how the exercise is to be carried out (see Figure 4.2 on page 44).

The driver will need to accelerate vigorously (subject to the power output of the vehicle) in order to attain a speed of 20/25 mph within the prescribed distance of 200 ft. When the front of the vehicle comes in line with the finishing cones the driver will be required to come off the accelerator and apply the footbrake firmly but without locking the wheels, keeping the footbrake depressed until the vehicle has come to an abrupt stop. The candidate must avoid locking the wheels, stalling the engine or in the case of articulated vehicles, jack-knifing the trailer.

To be sure that the exercises are carried out to the examiner's satisfaction, it is essential that they are practised over and over again on a suitable site before the candidate goes for test to ensure that they can be done correctly on the day of the test.

Vehicle and trailer

Where a candidate has brought an articulated vehicle for his driving test, an additional oral examination on the safe procedure affecting the coupling and uncoupling of the tractor unit and the semi-trailer will be included. For full details regarding these procedures, see Chapter 5.

The unified driving licence regulations indicate that a driver may bring a rigid vehicle and drawbar trailer for a driving test. At the time of writing there was no information available on how this will be handled from a licensing point of view, or on the exercises a driver may be required to perform with such a vehicle combination.

On the Road Driving

When the candidate has completed all the 'in-centre' manoeuvres and exercises, the driving examiner will direct him out of the test centre and onto the main road. The candidate will be told to follow the main road at all times unless told to do otherwise. In order to achieve success under test conditions it is essential that the driver concentrates on the job in hand and is not put off by the examiner's presence.

Under normal circumstances the driving examiner will make himself as inconspicuous as possible, thus allowing the driver the opportunity to concentrate and demonstrate the skills and abilities that lead to a good driving performance.

Figure 4.1
LGV and PCV
Manoeuvring Exercise – Reversing

The exercise is commenced from a position with the front of the candidate's vehicle in line with marker cones A and A1. The candidate reverses into the bay, keeping marker B on the offside, and stops with the extreme rear of his vehicle within the 3 ft. stopping area.

Distances   A – A1   = 1 ½ times width of vehicle.
             A – B   = 2 times length of vehicle.
             B – Line Z = 3 times length of vehicle.

The width of the bay will be 1½ times the width of the vehicle. The length of the bay will be based on the length of the vehicle, and, at the discretion of the examiner, will vary within the range: plus 3 ft. minus 6 ft.

The precise length of the bay will not be disclosed to the candidate before completing the exercise.

• indicates 18" marker cone.
• indicates 18" marker cone with 5 ft. coloured pole.

X = where the driver will position his vehicle prior to the exercise.

Figure 4.2
LGV and PCV
Braking Exercise

You will be allowed a distance of about 200 ft. in which to attain a speed of about 20 miles an hour; at the end of this distance a marker will show where you should begin to apply your brakes. The examiner will ride in the vehicle and will judge your ability to bring the vehicle to rest from about 20 miles an hour as quickly as possible, with safety and under complete control.

In good conditions, a well maintained goods vehicle in the hands of a competent driver should stop in the following distances from 20 mph:

Up to 4 tons unladen weight: 20 ft.
Up to 6 tons unladen weight: 25 ft.
Up to 10 tons unladen weight: 35 ft.

Make sure that the vehicle you bring for the test has good brakes. If you cannot stop within a reasonable distance when carrying out this exercise the examiner may decide to stop the test there and then in the interests of public safety; in which case you will lose your test fee.

Remember that if you apply excessive pressure on the brake pedal in an empty vehicle you may lock the wheels. This may increase your stopping distance and with an articulated vehicle may cause it to 'jack-knife'.

During the driving test the driving examiner will quietly assess the driver's ability on all types of roads and in all different traffic conditions. Particular attention will be paid to the driver having complete control of the vehicle throughout the whole of the test and to his ability to display courtesy and consideration to all other road users at all times. It is essential to drive the vehicle safely and progressively while adhering to all the rules of the road.

The driver must be able to adjust his driving to suit the different road conditions and also the different weather conditions. During the course of the test the examiner will ask the driver to perform various road exercises and procedures such as, gear changing, stopping and moving off and hill starts.

The driver must display confidence while driving, particularly when negotiating right turns, left turns, roundabouts and traffic lights, etc. You do not have to be a good driver in order to pass the driving test but you do have to be a safe driver. In order to assess your driving ability, one of the first exercises the examiner will ask you to perform will be to stop the vehicle at the side of the road and then to move away again safely.

Stopping Procedure

When the instruction 'pull up at a convenient place on the left' is given, the driving examiner will expect you to:

(a) observe and assess the situation ahead and select a safe parking position for your vehicle;

(b) observe the situation behind in your rear view mirrors and act accordingly in relation to what you see in them;

(c) to give the correct signal clearly and in good time;

(d) slow your vehicle down gradually in a safe and convenient manner and not stop your vehicle abruptly or extend the slowing down process over an excessive distance;

(e) bring your vehicle to rest close to and parallel to the kerb in a safe, legal and convenient position.

Once the vehicle has stopped, you should put the hand brake in the 'on' position and then put the gear lever into neutral and cancel your signal. It will not be necessary to stop your engine. Your driving examiner will normally acknowledge the stop and then ask you to move the vehicle off from this position.

Moving Off

In order to demonstrate the correct way of moving off, the driving examiner will expect you to:

(a) look in both mirrors and react sensibly to what you see in them;

(b) select the correct gear for moving off according to the gradient;

(c) give the correct signal in good time;

(d) physically look all round checking the necessary blind spots.

Move off only when it is safe to do so and under no circumstances should you move off if, by doing so, you cause other road users to take evasive action.

Uphill/On the Level

Moving off on an uphill gradient demands smooth co-ordination in the use of the accelerator, clutch and handbrake and it is very important in getting a LGV on the move. You must avoid using excessive engine revolutions or clutch slipping except on the steeper gradients, and under no circumstances should the vehicle be allowed to roll back.

Moving Off Downhill

If you are asked to move off on a down gradient, make sure that you demonstrate the correct procedure.

(a) mirrors as previously described;

(b) select the *correct* gear – this may be one gear higher than normal;

(c) apply the foot brake;

(d) release the hand brake, holding the vehicle firmly on the foot brake;

(e) signal as previously described;

(f) look all round as previously described;

(g) release the foot brake allowing the vehicle to roll forward and at the same time bring the clutch into play taking up the drive;

(h) move only when it is safe to do so.

Moving Off at an Angle

In order to move your vehicle off at an angle, the driving examiner will first ask you to 'pull up at a convenient place on the left, just before reaching a parked vehicle'. As you pull up behind a parked vehicle, be mindful of the fact that you will have to move off again and you must leave yourself sufficient room to do so.

The procedure that should be adopted when moving off will be determined by the gradient. If you are moving off on the flat or uphill you should move off using the hand brake as normal. If you are moving off on a down gradient you should move off using the foot brake. Naturally the examiner will expect you to take all the other precautions such as looking round, signalling as required and maintaining a professional smoothness on the vehicle controls.

Extra care is required not to get too close to the parked vehicle, allowing plenty of room for the cut-in from your own vehicle – particularly the trailer in the case of an articulated vehicle. Extra care must also be taken so as not to inconvenience any other road user as you move out from the nearside to the offside as you move out to pass the parked vehicle.

Gear Changing Exercise

In normal driving with most large goods vehicles, it would be unusual for a driver to use first gear when moving off. However, in order to demonstrate that you are able to engage any of the low gears when necessary, the driving examiner will require you to perform a gear changing exercise. This is usually conducted early on in the test. The driving examiner will direct you to a suitable road where this part of the test can be conducted with a minimum of inconvenience to other traffic. At the appropriate time you will be asked to pull up at a convenient place on the left, after which the driving examiner will give you very clear instructions as to what he requires you to do. Normally you will be asked to move off in the lowest gear on the vehicle and to drive for a reasonable distance in that gear before changing up into the next higher gear and so on until the examiner feels that you have engaged sufficient upward gears for the next part of the exercise to begin. He will then ask you to change down through each gear progressively until the lowest gear has once again been engaged.

It will not be necessary in this exercise to demonstrate the use of any auxiliary transmission systems, ie splitter box or two-speed axles (a splitter box should not be confused with a range change). You may use the foot brake as necessary to slow the vehicle down before any downward gear change.

Arm Signals

Signals given by arm are not included as a separate part of the test. However, candidates will be expected to give arm signals when required, ie at pedestrian crossings and as confirmation signals, and may be asked to demonstrate certain arm signals at the end of the test during the oral examination.

Primary Failure Points

Only by examining numerous Failure sheets will the primary failure points be revealed. Experience has shown that the most common failure points are:

  (a) Act correctly at road junctions.
  (b) Make proper use of gears.
  (c) Make proper use of mirrors.

Close examination of these points suggests that this is an area in which failures are more apparent. Candidates should be mindful of this fact and consider very carefully the following:

  Acting correctly at road junctions involves three stages:

  (a) The approach to them.
  (b) The negotiation of them.
  (c) The departure from them.

Each stage possesses its own individual failure points and will be scrutinised closely by the examiner.

The Approach

When approaching any type of road junction including crossroads and roundabouts, driving examiners will be observing that:

(a) The *mirrors* are used properly and that candidates act sensibly in relation to what they see in them.

(b) *Signals* are used (if required) and that they are given correctly, clearly and in good time.

(c) The vehicle is (if necessary) *manoeuvred* safely into the correct position.

Once the position has been attained, driving examiners will judge the candidate's ability to regulate the speed of the vehicle and, at the same time, assess the use of the brakes and gears as the final stage of the approach is completed. (It is this part of the approach which proves the most difficult, and where a large number of candidates have problems.)

The Negotiation

Negotiating road junctions involves a particular sequence of events which in the main will include:

(a) Proper observation before emerging or turning, including the use of the nearside *mirror* when about to turn left. *Particular attention should be paid to the nearside mirror when about to negotiate roundabouts,* and care should be taken to ensure that the cut-in of the large LGV does not endanger other road users.

(b) Emerging or turning safely with due regard for approaching traffic, not forgetting that a LGV is generally slower moving and larger than most other vehicles and this must be taken into account.

(c) Correct positioning of the vehicle throughout the negotiation. Depending upon the size of the vehicle, examiners will allow some degree of tolerance in positioning, but care must be taken not to endanger or inconvenience any other road users.

(d) Proper use of *mirrors* and all-round observation.

(e) Securing the correct road position for the vehicle when the negotiation/turn has been completed.

Changing *gear* on the turn is accepted, providing that it is done when the steering wheel is held firmly on course. *Do not* change gear *and* turn the wheel at the same time, and avoid crossing your hands on the wheel.

The Departure

The ingredients of a good departure from any road junction will include:

(a) A straight pre-planned course.

(b) Sound acceleration in accordance with road and traffic conditions.

(c) *Proper use of the gears,* each gear to be fully used before changing into the next higher gear.

(d) *Constant use of mirrors* throughout the departure.

(e) A watchful eye all round including the speedometer and rev counter.

Other Major Failure Points

(a) *'Exercise proper care in the use of speed'*: this simply means that the candidate drove too fast, either by breaking the legal speed limit or more often than not, by driving through low speed situations much too fast.

(b) *'Make normal progress to suit varying road and traffic conditions'*: this implies that the candidate drove too slowly throughout the whole of the test, but this is not always the case. It can include situations such as the candidate stopping unnecessarily at road junctions or roundabouts, failing to recognise and take advantage of a safe gap in traffic in order to emerge, or failing to take advantage of the opportunity to accelerate away from a hazard (as described in the discussion of the departure).

(c) *'Make proper use of gears'* (other than at road junctions): this usually means the driver has changed up a gear too early when the vehicle has not reached the correct speed for the next higher gear, changed up a gear too late where the vehicle's speed and road conditions are right for the next higher gear but the driver does not change up, selected the wrong gears eg by changing gear from 2nd to 3rd, missing 3rd and accidentally selecting another gear (not to be confused with block changing).

(d) *'Make proper use of mirrors'* (other than at road junctions): this is of the utmost importance and must be used often throughout the whole test. There is a right way and a wrong way to use mirrors and the driving examiner will observe if the candidate is using them correctly, eg using the right mirror at the right time. When you are about to drive round a right bend *you should check the offside mirror* as you do so as this will afford a far superior view of the road behind than the nearside mirror would. Likewise, when you are about to drive round a left hand bend you should use the *nearside mirror* as this will not only afford a better view of the road behind but will also allow you to see where the end of your vehicle is in relation to the kerb. This is particularly important in the case of articulated vehicles.

Obviously mirrors should be used before any change of direction no matter how slight and before signalling, moving off or stopping.

When negotiating a left turn at a road junction, you must look in the nearside mirror to check the back wheels of your vehicle in relation to the kerb, to ensure all is well behind and that there are no cyclists or pedestrians. When you are about to overtake a parked vehicle, you should look in the offside mirror first to ensure it is safe to move out (do not forget the signal if necessary) and then check the nearside mirror when you have passed the parked vehicle before returning to the nearside.

There are many examples to show how to use mirrors correctly but these can be summed up as:

- use mirrors often and react sensibly to what you see in them;
- use the correct mirror at the right time to make the best use of them.

Test Routes

LGV driving test routes have been carefully selected to include a large variety of driving conditions. You must be able to adjust your driving to suit the different conditions which you *will* encounter under test conditions. You will be given the opportunity to demonstrate your driving skills at high speeds one moment, then you will have to change your style of driving altogether the next moment as you are directed through a congested town centre. A test route is designed to test the ability of the driver and should never be under-estimated. As the driving part of the test nears completion, the examiner will direct you in a roundabout way back to the test centre where the final part of the test will be conducted.

Oral Examination

The final part of the driving test will be the oral examination which will be carried out in the vehicle when the candidate returns to the test station. Here he will be required to answer questions put to him by the examiner. The questions will be based on the Highway Code, vehicle safety and the recognition of selected road signs.

Highway Code

Questions asked by examiners follow no particular pattern and they can in fact be taken from *any* part of the Highway Code. However, it is certain that some of the questions asked will arise out of the way the candidate was driving earlier in the test. For example, if the candidate was asked to pull up on the left (and stop) and he did so opposite a parked vehicle or too close to a junction, then he will most certainly be asked, 'Where should you not stop or park a vehicle?'. The candidate would be ill advised, in his answer, not to include, among the many places where a driver should not stop or park his vehicle – 'opposite a parked vehicle or within 10 metres of a road junction'.

It will not be necessary to be able to recite the Highway Code word for word but a complete and comprehensive knowledge of it is essential.

About ten questions from the Highway Code will be asked, although it is not unusual for candidates to be asked more or less than this at the examiner's discretion. A selection of Highway Code questions and answers can be found on pages 93–8.

Vehicle Safety Questions

In order to test the candidate's knowledge of the components which affect the safe control of the vehicle, driving examiners are obliged to ask certain questions about the vehicle which is used for the test.

If the vehicle has not been fitted with any ancillary equipment such as a two-speed axle or power-assisted steering, this does not mean that candidates will be exempt from answering questions about them; on the contrary, the reverse may be true. A comprehensive list of questions and answers regarding vehicle safety has been included on pages 99–102.

Recognition of Road Signs

A selection of road signs and markings will be shown to the candidate and although a word perfect answer is preferred, it is not essential as long as the meanings are clear. In addition to the recognition of signs and markings, candidates may be required to answer questions on selected road signs and markings such as 'Where are you most likely to find the sign TWO-WAY TRAFFIC CROSSES ONE-WAY ROAD?' The answers to questions like this can be found in Chapters 8 and 9.

Completion of Test

On completing the test, successful candidates will be handed a Pass Certificate, which means that it is no longer necessary to be accompanied by a qualified driver or to display 'L' plates. The Pass Certificate and full ordinary licence together entitle candidates to drive LGVs of the category shown on the Pass Certificate, until such time as the provisional entitlement expires.

Statement of Failure

Failing a LGV driving test has been described as the worst feeling in the world and in my considered opinion there are only two ways a candidate can fail:

1. The candidate was not good enough to pass in the first place and had been entered for the test too early and needs more practice and more miles behind the wheel to gain the experience and confidence required.
2. The candidate was good enough to pass the test but made a mistake serious enough to warrant a failure. Anyone taking any type of test runs this risk no matter how good they are.

Where a driver has failed the test, he will be handed a Statement of Failure Guidance Notes. Matters requiring special attention will be marked accordingly and your driving examiner will allow a few minutes to explain the driving errors shown on the statement.

Should a driver have difficulty in understanding the driving errors shown on the Guidance Notes or if the driver feels that the test was unfairly conducted he may write to the Supervising Examiner (Driving Test) at the DVLA.

It is no longer necessary for unsuccessful candidates to wait a full calendar month before applying for another test.

Popular Misconceptions

There are many misconceptions about the LGV driving test and it is the intention of this section to clarify some of these by answering some of the many questions asked by those who are about to take the driving test; the principal object being to give the candidate a better understanding of the driving test and the examiner's aims.

Q. *What are driving examiners looking for?*
A. A safe, progressive drive with all the rules of the road adhered to.

Q. *Do you have to be a good driver to pass?*
A. No, but you do have to be a safe driver and be sure of what you are doing. Good driving comes with experience.

Q. *Will the examiner try to catch me out by asking me to turn into a road marked 'No Entry', etc?*
A. Absolutely not. Driving examiners are responsible people and will most certainly not try to catch out or trick a candidate during a test. On the contrary, the reverse is true and driving examiners can be very helpful.

Q. *Do drivers have to wear seat belts when taking a LGV driving test?*
A. It is not compulsory for drivers of LGVs to wear seat belts.

Q. *Can a driver take a shunt when doing the reversing exercises?*
A. A driver can take as many shunts as it takes in order to complete the exercise but he must be mindful of the fact that a properly prepared driver will complete the exercise without shunting.

Q. *Would a driver fail the test for taking say one shunt when reversing?*
A. Shunting is considered a minor fault and on its own will not fail a test but if in the opinion of the examiner the driver cannot reverse his vehicle safely then even a single shunt would result in failure.

Q. *If I knock a cone down or run over one during the reversing exercise will I fail?*
A. Knocking down or running over cones on the manoeuvring area is a serious fault and driving examiners could fail the candidate for such a fault – remember it is far better to take a shunt to avoid a cone than to knock one over.

Q. *Would you explain the reason for having two examiners present during a test?*

A. Occasionally it will be necessary for a second examiner to be present during a driving test. This is usually a senior driving examiner acting as an onlooker. The reason for his presence is to ensure that test procedures and standards are being maintained. He has no influence over the test and will make himself as inconspicuous as possible.

Q. *Can you cross your hands on the steering wheel?*

A. The candidate should try and avoid this as driving examiners prefer the traditional 'push and pull' method.

Q. *If I stall the engine, will I fail?*

A. A single stall during normal driving is a minor fault and will not constitute a failure although a stall during the braking exercise is considered to be a serious fault and will probably contribute towards a failure.

Q. *How much warning will the examiner give regarding turnings?*

A. All instructions regarding turnings, manoeuvres and other exercises will be given very clearly and in plenty of time.

Q. *If I make a mess of my reverse, can I ask to do it again?*

A. Yes, you can ask but the examiner's answer will probably be – 'That will not be necessary'.

Q. *Is it true that examiners have to fail so many every day?*

A. Absolutely not – driving examiners will pass every candidate who proves himself to be a safe and competent driver.

Q. *Can you do a gear change when on the turn?*

A. Yes, providing the steering is set on course for the turn, but DO NOT attempt to change gear and turn the wheel at the same time.

Q. *If you make a serious mistake at the beginning of the test (serious enough to fail), will the examiner fail you there and then and not continue with the rest of the test or will he complete the full test?*

A. The candidate has paid for a full test and under normal circumstances will be given a FULL test. Only under exceptional circumstances where the candidate has demonstrated that his standard of driving is such that it has become a danger to other road users will the examiner cut short the test.

Q. *What will happen if the vehicle breaks down while on test?*

A. The test will be terminated, test fee forfeited and the candidate will have to re-apply for another test.

Q. *Do you have to pull up within a certain distance when doing the braking exercise?*

A. Yes – the stopping distance will depend upon the speed of the vehicle, the weight of the vehicle and the conditions of the road at the time. A table of stopping distances for both motor cars and LGVs is shown overleaf.

Q. *Which gear should be used when moving off?*
A. The correct gear ie a lower gear when moving off from an uphill gradient; a higher gear when moving off from a downhill gradient.

Q. *Do you have to double the clutch when changing gear?*
A. This will depend upon the type of gearbox fitted to the vehicle, but as a general rule the driver will be expected to demonstrate the procedure of doubling the clutch, particularly when engaging first gear.

Q. *Do you have to put the handbrake on every time you stop?*
A. No, a driver will be expected to use the handbrake correctly whenever it is necessary.

Q. *If the vehicle gets a puncture during the course of the test will the examiner expect me to change the wheel?*
A. The examiner will not expect you to change the wheel there and then as time will not normally allow. The test will be terminated. The candidate will lose his test fee and the examiner will make his own way back to the test centre.

Q. *What is meant by a 'walk back'?*
A. A 'walk back' is the term used to describe a situation where the driving examiner leaves the vehicle and makes his own way back to the test centre.

Q. *What will happen if I am involved in an accident during the driving test?*
A. There is no answer to this question. Everything depends on the type and seriousness of the accident.

Shortest Stopping Distances

On a dry road, a good car with good brakes and tyres and an alert driver, will stop in the distances shown. Remember these are the *shortest* stopping distances. Stopping distances increase greatly with wet and slippery roads, poor brakes and tyres and tired drivers.

mph	thinking distance	braking distance	overall stopping distance
20	20ft (6m)	20ft (6m)	40ft (12m)
30	30ft (9m)	45ft (14m)	75ft (23m)
40	40ft (12m)	80ft (24m)	120ft (36m)
50	50ft (15m)	125ft (38m)	175ft (53m)
60	60ft (18m)	180ft (55m)	240ft (73m)
70	70ft (21m)	245ft (75m)	315ft (96m)

In good conditions a well maintained goods vehicle in the hands of a competent driver should be able to stop in the following distances from about 20 miles per hour:

Up to 4 tons unladen weight	20 ft (6m)
Up to 6 tons unladen weight	25 ft (7.5m)
Up to 10 tons unladen weight	35 ft (37.5m)

Chapter 5

Coupling and Uncoupling Articulated Vehicles (Vehicle and Trailer Support Information)

There are two types of coupling systems that are used to connect semi-trailers to tractor units (as shown in Figure 5.1). Candidates taking the test in articulated vehicles will be expected to know all about the coupling and uncoupling procedures, and the various checks that are involved in the connecting and disconnecting of tractor and trailer.

Examiners will question candidates on the particular type of coupling system employed on the vehicle used for the test, but it will be an advantage to know something about the other type; both types are discussed as follows.

Coupling and Uncoupling

Candidates taking the test in articulated vehicles will be required to answer questions put to them by the examiner in order to test their knowledge of coupling and uncoupling procedures. The examination will be conducted within the confines of the test station, with the examiner and candidate usually standing alongside the vehicle. It is introduced early in the test, usually before the candidate goes out on to the road.

Examiners adopt a simple but sophisticated 'question and answer' technique, and it is important that the candidate answers only that which he has been asked eg if you are asked 'How would you uncouple a semi-trailer from the tractive unit?', answer only that question. Any precautions or checks that must be made beforehand may be raised in separate questions at a later stage.

As this is a verbal exercise and not a practical one, it is important that the candidate can point out and explain the various components connected with the coupling and uncoupling of articulated vehicles. Experience has shown that a lot of potential drivers of articulated vehicles have difficulty in expressing themselves to an examiner's satisfaction. Therefore, it is advisable that the verbal procedures, checks and explanations are practised with a friend several times prior to the test.

If a semi-trailer is not connected properly to the tractive unit, the result could be disastrous. Therefore, it is strongly recommended that the checks and procedures are carried out, practically, several times under the keen eye and supervision of a qualified person.

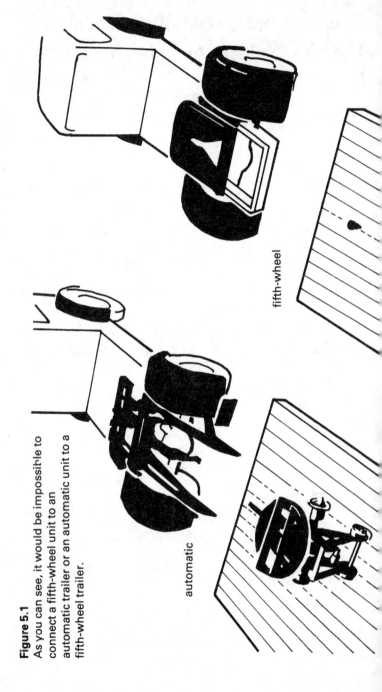

Figure 5.1
As you can see, it would be impossible to connect a fifth-wheel unit to an automatic trailer or an automatic unit to a fifth-wheel trailer.

fifth-wheel

automatic

Fifth-wheel Couplings

There are many components used in the connecting and disconnecting of semi-trailers to tractor units and in the interests of public and personal safety (as well as in passing the LGV test), it is essential that one is familiar with the main components, their functions, their locations, and their names.

The *trailer parking brake* is one such component, usually located on the nearside (left-hand) of the semi-trailer close to but forward of the trailer wheels – as shown in Figure 5.2. It is a mechanical cable brake that is applied manually and secures the trailer wheels. It is essential that it is put in the 'on' position whenever uncoupling takes place and, just as important, it must be set in the 'off' position immediately after coupling. It can also be used as an additional safety factor for overnight parking, or when leaving the vehicle on steep gradients.

The trailer support legs, commonly known as the *landing gear* (shown also in Figure 5.2), is the one component that is misused more than any other, and care should be taken when lowering the landing legs that they are stopped just short of the ground (about 1 inch). If the landing gear is forced hard down to the ground, strain and possibly damage may occur when recoupling, as the trailer is tugged forward (see below – *final exercise*).

Many landing gears are of a two-speed design. The high speed ratio is normally used for coupling and uncoupling purposes, but in exceptional circumstances it may be found necessary to lift or lower a detached trailer, which would necessitate using the low ratio.

The locking mechanism used to connect semi-trailers to tractor units is a combination affixed to both tractor and trailer.

The king pin is secured to a grease plate on the trailer while the *fifth-wheel* (sometimes known as the turntable) is fixed to the tractor. The actual locking mechanism is located inside the fifth-wheel, and to ensure proper connections it is important that drivers check the relative height between tractor and trailer before coupling commences. If the trailer is too high, not only is it possible for the king pin to damage the turntable, but also, and even more important, a false coupling could take place. The locking jaws in the fifth-wheel may have only partly gripped the king pin and although the trailer will move away with the unit, it is liable to disengage at any time without warning. As a safeguard against false coupling, the fifth-wheel is equipped with a locking bar and a safety catch. These components must be checked immediately after coupling to ensure the trailer is connected properly to the tractive unit.

The *final exercise* to be carried out to ensure a properly connected articulated vehicle is by selecting a low forward gear and, with the trailer brake still *on,* tug forward. IF YOU ARE IN ANY DOUBT, GET THE ADVICE AND ASSISTANCE OF A QUALIFIED PERSON.

Nylon air-coils, commonly known as the *air-lines*, were introduced in 1962. Since that time, air-coils have been fitted to 90% of all semi-trailers in this country. They overcame the disadvantages normally associated with the

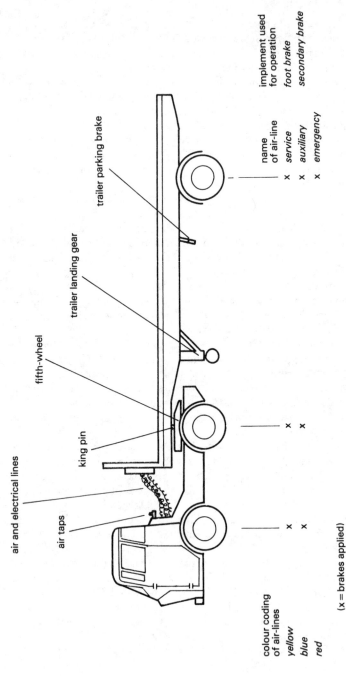

Figure 5.2 Colour coding of the three air-line braking system

rubber hose type air-line. All air-line coils are internationally colour coded (red, blue and yellow) and are capable of extending to at least such a length that they remain fully operational even when the articulated vehicle is in a complete jack-knife position. The function of the air-line is to carry compressed air from the tractor unit to the semi-trailer for the purpose of braking.

When disconnecting air-lines it is sensible to start with the one nearest to you and stow them away, one at a time. When connecting air-lines, start with the one furthest away and work towards you. This practice will reduce the risk of accidentally tripping over them, and help to keep the air-lines from tangling.

Figure 5.2 includes the colour coding of each air-line, the brakes that are applied through each line, the names by which the air-lines are known, and the implement used for their operation.

Most articulated vehicles in the UK are equipped with standard *male/female adaptors,* which reduce the risk of wrongly connecting. Some, however, use 'palm-couplings' which are all alike, and great care must be exercised to ensure that connections are not 'mixed'. The colour coding previously described is the reliable key. Incorrect connections can render the trailer brakes inoperative.

Where *air taps* are fitted, it is important that they are turned off before disconnecting air-lines. If this is not done, it will result in immediate air loss from the red emergency line and will render the yellow service line and the blue auxiliary line ineffective when applied. It is equally important that the air taps are turned on after air-lines have been connected. If this is not done, it will leave the brakes on the trailer totally inoperable.

Where air taps are not fitted, non-return valves are substituted. These are located within the air brake system and air pressure is immediately shut off or on automatically as the air-line connections are connected or disconnected.

Automatic Couplings

Automatic tractors and trailers were at one time popular within the road haulage industry, but their carrying capacity and weight limitations could not keep pace with the increasing demand made by hauliers. As a result, the automatic trailer and tractor nowadays are few and far between.

Most of the main components' locations and functions are the same as those applicable to the fifth-wheel type articulated vehicle. The obvious difference between the two is the coupling and uncoupling mechanism (as shown in Figure 5.1). The turntable and landing gear are affixed to the trailer. This in itself can be a potential danger to an inexperienced driver. The worst danger can occur if the trailer is coupled or uncoupled at an angle to the tractor unit. It is therefore essential that the coupling mechanism on the trailer is correctly lined up prior to coupling or uncoupling. Another main feature of the automatic is the fact that it can be disconnected by a trip lever located within the unit by the driver's seat. Care should be taken that this lever is kept clear from anything or anyone who could accidentally activate the release mechanism.

The following pages offer sample questions, answers, explanations and additional information that will not only help in passing this part of the LGV test, but will also assist in the laying of the foundation to becoming a better and more informed driver.

Automatic couplings

Q. *How should you uncouple a semi-trailer (automatic)?*

A. Apply the trailer brake.

Climb up between unit and trailer and turn off the air taps if fitted.

Disconnect the air-lines and electrics and stow away.

Climb down, remove trailer number plate and stow it away safely in the cab.

Climb into the cab and release trailer connection.

Drive away slowly, making sure that the trailer settles safely without causing any damage.

Q. *What is the correct procedure for coupling up an automatic trailer?*

A. Check that the trailer brake is applied.

Reverse slowly, checking height and line of the trailer.

When the coupling engages, select a low gear and tug forward.

Leave the cab in a safe position and make a visual check on the coupling.

Climb up between the unit and trailer.

Connect air-lines.

Connect electrical line, if fitted.

Turn on the air taps, if fitted.

Climb down.

Release the trailer brake.

Fit the number plate.

Checks before coupling:

Ensure that the trailer coupling connection is at the correct angle.

Ensure that the trailer brake is on.

Ensure that the air-line connections on the trailer match the air-line connection on the unit.

Fifth-wheel Couplings

Q. *What is the correct procedure for coupling up to a fifth-wheel semi-trailer?*

A. Check that the trailer brake is on.

Climb into the cab and reverse slowly, checking relative heights of tractor and trailer and making sure that the unit is in line with the trailer.

Reverse until the coupling engages.

Select a low forward gear and tug forward.

When you are satisfied that the fifth-wheel is connected, climb down from the cab leaving it in a safe position.

Do a visual check on the fifth-wheel and ensure that the safety catch is on.

Climb up between the unit and trailer and connect air-lines and electrical line (turn on taps if fitted).

Climb down.

Raise landing gear and stow away the handle.

Take off the trailer brake.

Fix the number plate and carry out all checks.

Q. *What check would you make* **before** *you couple up to a semi-trailer?*

A. Trailer brake on, air-line connections are the same on the trailer as they are on the unit.

Q. *What check would you make* **after** *you have coupled up to a semi-trailer?*

A. Lights, brakes and tyres.

Q. *How should you uncouple a semi-trailer (fifth-wheel)?*

A. Apply the trailer brake.

Lower the handling gear and stow the handle away.

Climb up between the unit and the trailer.

Turn off the air taps (if fitted).

Disconnect the air-lines and electrics, stow away.

Climb down.

Remove the safety catch on the fifth-wheel and disconnect the fifth-wheel.

Retrieve the number plate from the trailer, stow it in the cab.

Get into the cab and drive away slowly, making sure that the trailer causes no damage as it settles.

Q. *What checks should be made* **before** *you uncouple a semi-trailer?*

A. Check that the ground where the trailer is to be uncoupled is firm, level and that the trailer will be in a safe position.

Q. *What checks would you make* **after** *you have uncoupled a semi-trailer?*

A. Check that the trailer brake is on.

Q. *What is the last thing to check before moving away when you have collected a trailer?*

A. Check that you have the correct number plate affixed to the trailer, and the trailer parking brake is in the off position.

Q. *What exercise should be taken to ensure that the king pin is securely locked when coupling?*

A. Engage a low forward gear and tug forward while the trailer brakes are still on.

Q. *With air brakes, why is it important that after uncoupling a semi-trailer you would go back to check that the trailer brake is on?*

A. The trailer brake is first put on manually but when the red emergency line is disconnected, all the brakes on the trailer come on automatically via air pressure. Air pressure being superior to manual effort, the trailer brakes would go on much harder and the cable brake would go slack.

Q. *How would you check the stop lights on a trailer if you were on your own?*
A. Via reflection or by placing a weighted object (jack) on to the foot brake.

Q. *What types of air-line connection are there?*
A. Male, female and palm couplings.

Q. *What is the colour coding of the air-lines and which brakes are applied through each line?*
A. RED = emergency, applies all brakes on the trailer.
BLUE = auxiliary, applies all brakes on the outfit.
YELLOW = service, applies all brakes on the outfit.

Coupling and Uncoupling Rigid Vehicle and Drawbar Trailer (Support Information)

The new unified driving licence regulations indicate that a driver *may* bring a rigid vehicle and drawbar trailer combination for a driving test. At the time of writing there was no information available regarding this. However, for support information only the correct procedures for coupling and uncoupling a drawbar trailer to the rigid prime mover are as follows.

Drawbar Outfits
The free standing drawbar requires a second person to ensure correct alignment. The pre-set aligning drawbar can be operated by the driver alone.

Uncoupling
Before uncoupling:

- Make sure that the ground where you are working is *firm and level.*
- Select a safe and sensible position for the trailer *before you start.*

To uncouple:

- Apply trailer brake
- Check trailer wheels
- Turn off air taps (if fitted)
- Disconnect air and electrical lines
- Remove safety pin and disconnect drawbar connection
- Put trailer number plate in cab
- Drive away slowly

After uncoupling:

- Check trailer brake

- Check trailer wheel chocks

Coupling

Before coupling:

- Ensure that trailer parking brake is *on*
- Ensure that wheel chocks are in place
- Ensure that drawbar is *in line with* the front of the trailer.

Coupling (two-man operation):

Driver

- Reverse slowly – know exactly *where your assistance is positioned*
- Minimise engine noise – you must be able to hear his instructions

Assistant

- As vehicle is reversed make sure that its coupling box is in line with the drawbar
- Tell the driver to stop as soon as the coupling connection is made
- Lock the coupling mechanism – and *stand clear*

Driver

- When you are sure that your assistant is clear of the vehicle select a low gear and tug forward to test coupling
- Stop – apply handbrake.

Assistant

- Connect air and electrical lines
- Turn on air taps (if fitted)
- Attach appropriate number plate to rear of trailer
- Remove wheel chocks
- Release trailer brake

After coupling:

- Check all tyres and lights (including indicators)
- Test brakes at earliest opportunity

Large Vehicle Trailers

1. A fifth wheel semi-trailer

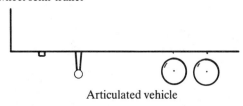

Articulated vehicle

2. An automatic semi-trailer

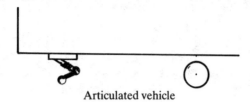

Articulated vehicle

3. A drawbar trailer

Rigid vehicle plus drawbar trailer

Chapter 6

The Passenger Carrying Vehicle (PCV) Driving Test

A driver who wishes to drive a large passenger vehicle (PCV) will need to pass a PCV driving test.

PCV driving tests are conducted at local test centres (at the same place where LGV driving tests are conducted).

The test will follow a similar format to the LGV driving test and potential PCV drivers will have to satisfy the driving examiner that he can drive the vehicle safely, competently and be able to demonstrate the various manoeuvres and exercises as required.

All the driving elements as previously mentioned for LGV are the same for PCV with only minor changes which relate specifically to vehicles that carry passengers.

Note: Candidates for the PCV test *must* give at least 21 days' notice before the test can be conducted. (This applies only to the first application.)

The Driving Test

The driving test will consist of four main elements:

1. A reversing exercise
2. A braking exercise } within the test centre
3. A driving demonstration (on the road)
4. An oral question and answer section.

Tests are arranged to a strict timetable and applicants must not be late for their appointment.

The vehicle used for the test *must*:

(a) display 'L' plates front and rear,
(b) be in a thoroughly roadworthy condition,
(c) display a valid vehicle excise licence,
(d) have a secure seat for the examiner to be suitably positioned close to the driver,
(e) allow the examiner a clear view of the road directly behind the vehicle without relying on mirrors,

    (f) allow the examiner to be able to speak to the applicant while he is driving,

    (g) have enough fuel for the duration of the test up to 1½ hours.

Unless the vehicle complies with all the above-mentioned requirements the examiner may refuse to conduct the test and the test fee will be forfeited.

Note: Drivers taking the test must be aware of the following:

    (a) the height, width, length and weight of the vehicle,

    (b) the position of the emergency fuel cut-off,

    (c) the position of all fire extinguishers.

Drivers must also make sure that all the doors are closed properly and that any equipment carried is in the right place and secured.

Reception

On arrival at the testing station the candidate will be required to park the vehicle in an appropriate parking place and report to the reception. At the appointed time the driving examiner will call upon the candidate to sign the examiner's test programme and then ask him to lead the way to his vehicle.

The reversing exercise. The first part of the driving test will be the reversing exercise which will take place on a special manoeuvring area within the confines of the test centre.

The candidate will be directed to the manoeuvring area and the driving examiner will give clear instructions as to how the driver should position the vehicle prior to the actual manoeuvre taking place.

This exercise will begin when the vehicle is in position at the bottom right-hand corner of the manoeuvring area whereupon the driving examiner will give clear instructions as to how the exercise is to be carried out (see Figure 4.1 on page 44). Great care must be taken when doing this exercise as there is very little margin for error. The driver who tends to over-steer or under-steer or fails to position the vehicle *correctly* or tends to reverse too fast or erratically, will undoubtedly bring pressure upon himself. The driver must position the vehicle correctly, use the accelerator, clutch and steering effectively, and maintain a slow but constant speed.

Ideally the candidate should be able to position the vehicle correctly and complete the exercise without having to stop or without having to take a shunt.

The braking exercise. The second part of the driving test is the braking exercise. Here the candidate will be directed to another part of the manoeuvring area where this exercise can be carried out. The candidate will be directed to the start line/position where he will be required to park his vehicle in order to allow the driving examiner to climb aboard. Only when the examiner has settled in and has secured all his paperwork will he give instructions as to how the exercise is to be carried out (see Figure 4.2 on page 44).

The driver will need to accelerate smoothly and progressively (subject to the power output of the vehicle) in order to attain a speed of 20/25 mph within the prescribed distance of 200 ft. When the front of the vehicle comes in line with the cones, the driver will be required to come off the accelerator and apply the footbrake firmly but without locking the wheels, keeping the footbrake depressed and stopping quickly but under full control. The candidate must avoid locking the wheels or stalling the engine.

To be sure that the exercises are carried out to the examiner's satisfaction it is essential that they are practised over and over again on a suitable site before the candidate goes for test to ensure that they can be done correctly on the day of the test.

On the road – when both exercises have been completed the candidate will be directed out of the test centre and will be given instructions to follow the road ahead at all times unless told to do otherwise.

During the course of normal driving the candidate will be required to perform a simulated stop at an authorised bus stop. Instructions regarding this exercise will be given and the candidate will be required to stop the vehicle at a pre-selected stopping place as though stopping at a bus stop.

The PCV gear changing exercise now falls in line with the gear exercise required from a driver undertaking the LGV driving test and will follow the same pattern as described on page 47.

Oral examination

When the driving part of the test has been completed the candidate will be directed back to the testing station where the oral examination will be carried out with both examiner and candidate seated in the vehicle. The examiner will ask the candidate a number of questions on:

(a) Highway code,
(b) recognition of selected road signs,
(c) questions affecting the safe control of the vehicle, and
(d) a selection of special PCV questions.

Examples of the types of questions asked on the Highway Code can be found on page 93, road signs identification on page 75 and vehicle safety questions on page 99. Some specimen questions on technical matters affecting vehicle safety applicable to PCV vehicles are listed below.

Q. *What items of equipment should be carried on some PCV services, express services, etc?*
A. First aid kit, fire extinguisher, a jack

Q. *Why is a jack part of the equipment?*
A. To raise vehicle should anyone become trapped

Q. *Describe the bell signals and what they mean?*
A. One, stop at the next stop; two, move away when safe; more than two, emergency stop

Q. *What are you not permitted to do when in charge of a PCV, but would be in order in any other vehicle?*
A. Smoke (even when at rest if there are passengers on board); talk with passengers when driving

Q. *Where should an identity disc (badge) be worn and for what purpose?*
A. So that it can be clearly seen, for anyone wishing to note the number from the centre of the badge

Q. *Where is the emergency exit situated on this vehicle?*
A. Describe where it is

Q. *How would you know if the emergency exit had been unlocked?*
A. Either warning light and/or buzzer in cab

Q. *Where is the emergency 'cut-off' on this vehicle?*
A. Describe where it is and how to operate it

Q. *What precautions should be taken during the removal and replacement of the road wheels when carrying passengers?*
A. Empty the vehicle of passengers and keep them clear of the vehicle. Select a firm surface on the level. Apply the parking brake and scotch the road wheels.

When the driving test has been completed, successful candidates will be handed a DLP 23 Pass Certificate which must then be sent to the DVLA, after which a licence and badge will be issued. Unsuccessful candidates will be handed a DLP 24 Statement of Failure. Candidates wishing to re-take the test may re-apply and it will not be necessary to wait one calendar month.

A candidate may drive for 4 weeks without a PCV licence after passing the driving test.

Note: Passengers must not be carried during training or during the driving test.

Chapter 7

Waiting, Parking, Loading and Unloading: Restrictions

There are many rules and regulations concerning waiting, parking, loading and unloading and it is essential for drivers of LGVs to be familiar with these rules in order to be able to answer questions about them during the oral part of the driving test and to be able to carry out the duties of a LGV driver.

Loading and Unloading Restrictions

Yellow markings (stripes) painted on the kerb or at the edge of carriageways indicate no loading or unloading. A plate situated nearby will qualify the times of the prohibition. If no days are indicated on the sign, the restrictions are in force every day, including Sundays and Bank Holidays.

For example:

One Stripe
No loading or unloading during times stated on the qualifying plate (usually peak periods).

```
No loading
Mon-Fri
8·00-9·30am
4·30-6·30pm
```

For example:

Two Stripes
No loading or unloading during a working day.

```
No loading
Mon-Sat
8·30am-6·30pm
```

For example:

Three stripes
No loading or unloading during a working day and additional times.

```
No loading
at any time
```

Note: If it is necessary to make a delivery or a collection where kerb-marking restrictions are in force, prior permission from the police should be obtained.

Waiting and Parking Restrictions

Yellow markings (lines) painted along the gutter area of the road or carriageway indicate no waiting. A plate situated nearby will qualify the times of the prohibition. HOWEVER, THIS DOES NOT PREVENT LOADING OR UNLOADING. If no days are indicated on the sign, the restrictions are in force every day including Sundays and Bank Holidays. The lines give a guide to the restriction in force but the time plates must be consulted.

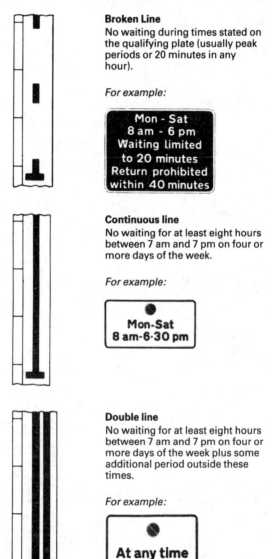

Broken Line
No waiting during times stated on the qualifying plate (usually peak periods or 20 minutes in any hour).

For example:

> Mon - Sat
> 8 am - 6 pm
> Waiting limited
> to 20 minutes
> Return prohibited
> within 40 minutes

Continuous line
No waiting for at least eight hours between 7 am and 7 pm on four or more days of the week.

For example:

> Mon-Sat
> 8 am-6·30 pm

Double line
No waiting for at least eight hours between 7 am and 7 pm on four or more days of the week plus some additional period outside these times.

For example:

> At any time

Waiting restrictions indicated by yellow lines and time plates apply to all vehicles, but in some areas local authorities are introducing special goods vehicle waiting restrictions, often in conjunction with lorry parks. Usually these apply to goods vehicles over two tons unladen weight.

Where the restriction applies throughout a zone, **zone entry signs** mark the limits of the restricted area.

Zone exit sign

Entrance to controlled parking zone

End of controlled parking zone

These signs will replace existing signs.

Loading and Unloading in a Waiting Restricted Area

A driver may stop his vehicle where a waiting restriction is in force for the purpose of loading or unloading only. Under such circumstances, a time limit of 20 minutes is normally allowed (although this is not shown on the qualifying plate). Should extra time be required to complete the operation, then prior permission from the police should be obtained. When loading or unloading is not taking place, the waiting restrictions must be observed.

Parking Meters

Vacant parking meter bays can be used for the purpose of loading or unloading for up to 20 minutes without charge. However, a police officer or a traffic warden has the right to move you on.

Parking Restrictions

It is an offence to leave a vehicle unattended with the engine running (except for the purpose of using ancillary equipment). Trailers and semi-trailers must not be left by the side of the road or in lay-bys, detached from the prime mover. Unless authorisation has been given by a police officer in uniform and the vehicle is then not left unattended, it is also an offence to park a motor vehicle, wholly or partly (unless signs show otherwise) on:

(a) the verge,
(b) footway, or
(c) the central reservation of an urban road.

Break-down in Restricted Areas and Subsequent Removal of Vehicle

Should your vehicle break down where a waiting restriction is in force and it is necessary for you to leave it unattended to summon assistance, you should notify the police or a traffic warden. The police are empowered to remove *any* vehicle which is causing an obstruction or is left in a dangerous position or is contravening waiting, loading and unloading restrictions.

Parking without Lights

Goods vehicles not exceeding 1525 kg unladen may be parked at night without lights on roads provided that:

(a) the road is subject to a 30 mph speed limit or less,
(b) the vehicle is parked close to the kerb and parallel to it, and except in a one-way street, with its nearside to the kerb,
(c) no part of the vehicle is within 10 metres of a road junction,
(d) there are no parking restrictions in force at the time.

Goods vehicles over this weight must always display lights when parked on a road at night.

Clamp-down Parking

Clamp-down parking has been introduced in various parts of the country.

Where certain parking restrictions are consistently being abused, the police will clamp and lock large metal wheel plates to the offending vehicle which will prevent it from being used. The owner of the vehicle will have to report to a police station in order to have the plate removed.

Should this practice prove to be successful, clamp-down parking may be adopted in other parts of the country.

Chapter 8

Traffic Signs

A wide range of traffic signs which have been gradually introduced on our roads are illustrated here. All will be relevant to the driving of LGVs.

STOP sign
Stop and give way.

Mini roundabout
Give way to traffic from the immediate right.

Loose chippings

Staggered junction

This and other versions of junction signs indicates the priority through the junction by the thickened line.

T-junction

Crossroad

Side road

Tunnel

Indicates the road ahead entering a tunnel – look out for head room.

Steep hill down

The gradient should be included on this sign. The sign is often accompanied by a plate: 'low gear now'.
Gradients may also be shown as a ratio, ie 20% = 1:5

Steep hill up

On relatively steep hills on motorways an extra lane is sometimes provided so that slow-moving vehicles need not impede faster traffic.

The **bus lane sign** and **road marking**
In some towns specific traffic lanes may be reserved for buses. Goods vehicles may cross the white line and enter the bus lane to stop to load or unload goods, but only at times when there is no restriction on loading.

An **advance direction sign** may indicate a restriction and offer an alternative route.

Lorry parks
The Department of the Environment was encouraging the setting-up of a national network of secure lorry parks with accommodation for drivers and other approved facilities. As the department is no longer extending the network, only a limited number of these signs are in use.

Advisory lorry routes
Where a port or an industrial centre is not directly on a primary route the white lorry symbol may be used to mark the most suitable route for LGVs to and from the primary route.

No vehicle or combination of vehicles over length shown

No vehicles (including load) over weight shown (in tonnes)

No goods vehicles over maximum gross weight shown (in tonnes)

Axle weight limit in tonnes

No vehicles over width shown

No vehicles with over 12 seats except regular scheduled school and works buses

No vehicles over height shown

End of goods vehicle restriction

Warning Signals near Railways

At automatic half-barrier level crossings drivers of large or slow vehicles *must* telephone both before and after crossing.

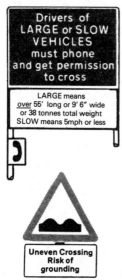

'Large' means over 55' long or 9'6" wide or 38 tonnes total weight. 'Slow' means 5mph or less.

Where there is danger of grounding you may see this warning sign at the last road junction before the crossings and on the approaches to these and other types of crossing. Drivers of vehicles with low ground clearance should not try to cross until they have made sure that there is no risk of grounding on the crossing. *If in doubt drivers should telephone the signalman* – or speak to him direct if he is at the crossing.

Overhead electric cables
The plate indicates the maximum safe height for vehicles.

'Count-down' markers approaching a concealed level crossing. Each bar represents one third of the distance from the warning sign to the crossing.

At an open level crossing

Hump bridge

Hump bridge

Risk of grounding of long low vehicles at level crossing

Level crossing without barrier
(the additional lower half of the cross is used when there is more than one railway line)

Overhead Warning Signals on Motorways

Mounted above and applicable to each lane.

Flashing red signal.
Do not proceed any further in this lane

Change lane

Leave the motorway at the next exit

Temporary maximum speed

End of restriction

81

Roadside Warning Signals on Motorways

These signals are situated on the central reserve at intervals of not more than two miles and they apply to all lanes.

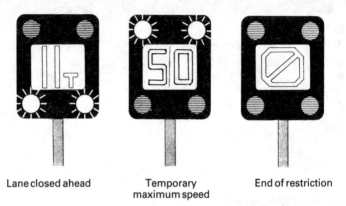

Lane closed ahead   Temporary   End of restriction
maximum speed

Diversions from Motorways

It is sometimes necessary, because of emergencies, to close either one or both carriageways of a motorway. When this is done, special signs will sometimes be shown to tell drivers on the motorway (or those wanting to join it) about the alternative route they should follow. This route will guide them back to the motorway beyond the point of closure.

The diversion sign could be part of an existing direction sign or a separate sign on its own. If the diversion route is easy to identify and follow, the signs will show only its route number (for example A38 via Bridgewater) and there will be no additional diversion signs along this route. This is a typical sign:

Sometimes there are too many route numbers to show on the diversion sign, or the alternative route may not have a route number. In such cases the diversion route will be indicated by symbols of various shapes shown on the diversion sign and along the recommended route. The symbol may be a rectangle, a circle, a triangle or a diamond and each of these may be either black, or yellow with a thick black border, for example:

On a motorway diversion sign the symbol will be like this:

Along the diversion (alternative) route, drivers should look for the symbol which will be shown on the traffic direction signs which will guide them back to the motorway. Along the route, the symbols will be like this:

Where two or more diversion routes cross or follow the same length of road, different symbols will be used to avoid confusion. Therefore, if you should be diverted from a motorway by a sign which shows one of these symbols, keep a good look out for the coloured symbol along the alternative route and always follow the correct symbol.

Chapter 9
Traffic Signs Test

Each of the following traffic signs is accompanied by a statement, an alternative or a question. Check your answers against those given at the foot of each page.

(1)
Light signals on urban motorways
A. Change lane
B. Leave motorway

(2)
A. No pedestrians
B. Pedestrians in road ahead

(3)
Height limit
What is the minimum height of an unmarked bridge?

(4)
A. Pedestrian crossing
B. No pedestrians

(5)
A. Danger – cross winds
B. Location of level crossing without gates or barriers

(6)
A. Temporary STOP sign
B. Stop and give way

(7)
A. Pedestrian crossing
B. Children

(8)
A. Maximum speed limit
B. Minimum speed limit

(9)
A. Cattle grid
B. Level crossing with barrier or gate

(10)
A. End of maximum speed limit
B. End of minimum speed limit

(11)
A. Contra-flow bus lane
B. Bus lane

(12)
What are the maximum speed limits for LGVs where this sign is displayed?

(13)
A. Hump back bridge
B. Uneven road

(14)
A. Uneven road
B. Hump back bridge

(15)
Two-way traffic crosses a one-way road
Give two places where you may find this sign

(16)
A. Minimum speed limit
B. Maximum speed limit

Answers: (7)B (8)A (9)B (10)B (11)A (12) 40 mph ordinary road, 50 mph dual carriageway (60 mph on a motorway) (13)B (14)B (15) At the T-junction end of a dual carriageway and/or a one-way street (16)A

(17)
A. Right-hand lane closed
B. No right turn

(18)
A. Axle weight limit
B. Total weight limit

(19)
A. Turn left ahead
B. Turn left

(20)
What does this sign mean?

(21)
A. No entry
B. No vehicles

(22)
A. School crossing patrol
B. Pedestrian crossing ahead

(23)
A. No vehicles with more than 12 seats
B. Passenger service vehicles only

(24)
A. Turn left ahead
B. Turn left

(25)
What does this sign mean?

(26)
A. T-junction
B. No through road

Answers: (17)A (18)A (19)B (20) Parking place. Additional plate indicates lorry park
(21)B (22)A (23)A (24)A (25) No entry for vehicular traffic (26)B

(27)
A. Steep hill upwards
B. Steep hill downwards

(28)
What does this sign mean?

(29)
A. Traffic merges from the left
B. Give way to traffic from the right

(30)
A. Opening bridge
B. Quayside or river bank

(31)
A. Traffic merges from right
B. Traffic merges from left

(32)
A. Slippery road
B. Series of bends

(33)
What does this sign mean?

(34)
A. Falling rocks
B. Falling or fallen rocks

(35)
A. Two-way traffic
B. Pass either side

(36)
A. Low-flying aircraft or sudden noise
B. Stop – aircraft landing

Answers: (27)B (28) End of motorway (29)A (30)A (31)A (32)A (33) Steep hill upwards (34)B (35)B (36)A

(37)
A. Double bend
B. Overhead power cables

(38)
Continuous prohibition plate
A. No waiting at any time
B. No stopping at any time (clearway)

(39)
A. Level crossing without gates or barriers
B. Location of level crossing without gates or barriers

(40)
A. T-junction
B. Side road

(41)
A. Road across water
B. Water

(42)
A. Cyclists only
B. Cycling prohibited

(43)
A. Quayside or river bank
B. Opening or swing bridge

(44)
A. Deep pot holes
B. Loose chippings

(45)
A. Minimum head room
B. No vehicles over height shown

(46)
A. Staggered junction
B. Cross-roads

Answers: (37)B (38)A (39)B (40)B (41)B (42)B (43)A (44)B (45)B (46)A

(47)
A. Route for pedal cyclist only
B. No route for pedal cyclist

(48)
What does this sign mean?

(49)
A. Series of bends
B. Double bend

(50)
A. No stopping (clearway)
B. No waiting

(51)
A. No vehicles
B. No motor vehicles

(52)
A. Priority over vehicles from opposite direction
B. Give priority to vehicles from opposite direction

(53)
A. Keep right
B. Mini roundabout

(54)
A. No overtaking
B. Two-way traffic straight ahead

(55)
A. No vehicles over 7.5 tonnes
B. No vehicles under 7.5 tonnes

(56)
A. Give priority to vehicles from opposite direction
B. Priority over vehicles from opposite direction

Answers: (47)A (48) Entrance to a controlled parking zone (49)B (50)A (51)B (52)A (53)B (54)B (55)A (56)A

(57)
A. Railway line ahead
B. Ring-road

(58)
A. Bus lane ahead
B. Bus lane at junction ahead

(59)
A. Road narrows on both sides
B. End of dual carriageway

(60)
What does this sign mean?

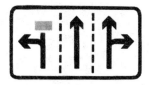

(61)
A. Traffic lanes at a junction
B. No left turn

(62)
A. Change lane
B. Change to opposite carriageway

(63)
A. Stop and give way
B. Give way to traffic on major road

(64)
A. End of dual carriageway
B. Road narrows from both sides

(65)
A. No overtaking
B. Two-way traffic

(66)
What does this sign mean?

Answers: (57)B (58)B (59)A (60)Holiday route (61)A (62)B (63)B (64)A (65)A (66)
End of controlled parking zone

(67)
A. Manually operated stop sign
B. Stop at junction

(68)
A. Goods vehicles prohibited
B. No vehicles over width shown

(69)
A. No vehicles over length shown
B. Heavy goods vehicles only

(70)
A. No pedestrians
B. Pedestrian crossing

(71)
A. Pedestrian crossing
B. No pedestrians

(72)
A. No vehicles over weight shown
B. Axle weight limit

(73)
A. Road clear
B. Other danger

(75)
A. Wild horses or ponies
B. Accompanied horses or ponies
    crossing the road ahead

(74)
What does this road marking mean?

Answers: (67)A (68)B (69)A (70)B (71)B (72)A (73)B (74) Warning of 'Give Way'
        junction ahead (75)B

Chapter 10

The Highway Code

Most of the questions asked in this section have been taken from the new Highway Code, and they offer an excellent example of the type of question likely to be asked during the oral part of the driving test. Driving examiners do not require word-perfect answers from the Highway Code as long as the explanation is clear.

Motorway Driving

Q. *LGVs must not use the third lane of a three-lane motorway. Give two exemptions to this rule, other than emergency circumstances.*
A. When passing a wide load or when passing roadworks.

Q. *Some motorways still have flashing amber signals at their entrances and at one or two-mile intervals. The lights warn of danger ahead when they are flashing and the Highway Code advises drivers to do what?*
A. Keep your speed to under 30 mph.

Q. *What is the maximum speed limit for LGVs on motorways?*
A. 60 mph.

Q. *What are the colours of the cats' eyes on motorways and in what positions are they?*
A. Amber – on the right-hand edge of the carriageway.
   Red   – on the left-hand edge of the carriageway.
   Green – at intersections.
   White – at lane lines.

Q. *If you go past your turn-off point, what must you do?*
A. Carry on until you reach the next exit point. Do not reverse or turn back.

Q. *If the lights above your lane are flashing red, what should you do?*
A. Stop.

Q. *Cross-winds on a motorway are a serious danger for high-sided vehicles; what action would you take if you were driving such a vehicle?*
A. Reduce speed and consider leaving the motorway.

Q. *What should you do if you break down on the motorway?*
A. Move onto the hard shoulder.

Q. *If, while driving on a motorway, you notice something fall on to the carriageway, what should be done?*

A. Inform the police. Do not try to retrieve it yourself.

Fog Code

Q. *What are the points to remember when driving in fog?*

A.   1. Check your mirrors and slow down.

      2. Do not hang on to someone else's tail lights.

      3. Watch your own speed and do not speed up to get away from a vehicle which is too close behind you.

      4. Heavy goods vehicles may take longer to pull up.

      5. Observe and obey warning signals.

      6. Use dipped headlamps or front fog lamps, use windscreen wipers and demisters.

      7. Check and clean windscreens, lights, reflectors and windows whenever you can.

      8. Be mindful that fog can drift rapidly.

      9. Take particular care when driving in fog after dark.

    10. Allow more time for the journey.

Level Crossings

Q. *If your vehicle breaks down when negotiating an automatic half-barrier level crossing, what must you do?*

A. Get your passengers out of the vehicle and clear of the crossing and ring the signalman.

Q. *Subject to what the signalman says and if there is time to move the vehicle, what efforts could you make to move your vehicle off the crossing?*

A. Try to push the vehicle off; failing that, put it into low gear, release the hand-brake and wind it off on the starter.

Q. *At some automatic half-barrier level crossings, there is a large rectangular sign (blue background with white letters) that says: 'Drivers of large or slow vehicles must phone and get permission to cross' – What is defined as 'large or slow'?*

A. Large – over 55 ft long or 9 ft 6 in wide or 38 tonnes total weight.
Slow – 5 mph or less.

Q. *What action should be taken when negotiating a level crossing without gates, attendant or warning lights?*

A. Stop, look both ways, listen and make sure there are no trains coming before you cross.

Q. *What is meant by grounding?*

A. The bottom of a trailer catching the peak of an uneven road surface, which may happen with certain types of trailer, eg a low loader.

Q. *If there is a danger of grounding, what sign may you see?*
A. Uneven road, hump back bridge with qualifying plates.

Q. *What must you never do at an automatic half-barrier level crossing when the barriers are down?*
A. Never zig-zag around the barriers.

Q. *If you are negotiating an automatic half-barrier level crossing when the red lights and bells start, what must you do?*
A. Keep going.

Q. *What are the general rules covering the use of all railway level crossings?*
A. 1. Approach at a moderate speed.
   2. Cross with care.
   3. Never drive nose to tail.
   4. Never drive onto the crossing unless you can see that the road is clear on the other side.
   5. Never stop on or immediately beyond any level crossing.
   6. Do not loiter.

Q. *If the barriers stay down at any time for more than three minutes without a train arriving, what should you do?*
A. Phone the signalman for advice.

Pedestrian Crossings

Q. *Why are zebra crossings marked with white zig-zag lines?*
A. To make them safer and more visible to oncoming traffic.

Q. *What must you not do at a zebra crossing marked with zig-zag lines?*
A. Do not wait or park on the zig-zags.
   Do not overtake the moving motor vehicle that is nearest to the crossing, or the leading vehicle which has stopped to give way to pedestrians on it.

Q. *What is the sequence of light signals at a pelican crossing, starting from red?*
A. Red – flashing amber – green – steady amber – red.

Q. *What does flashing amber mean?*
A. Give way to pedestrians who are already crossing, but if your way is clear, you may proceed.

Q. *Can you overtake a slow moving vehicle, eg milk float, on the far side of a zebra crossing that has been marked with zig-zag lines?*
A. Yes, but remember, do not overtake on the approach side of the crossing.

Road Markings

Q. *What are the rules governing the use of a box junction?*
A. Do not enter unless your exit is clear, except when you are turning right and are prevented from doing so by oncoming traffic.

Q. *What are the rules governing double white lines in the centre of the road?*
A. You must not stop where there are double white lines in the centre of the road. Where the line nearest to you is broken, you may cross it providing it is safe to do so, but where the line nearest to you is continuous, you must not cross it except in special circumstances.

Q. *Can you park your vehicle alongside double white lines if the line nearest to you is broken?*
A. No.

Q. *Under special circumstances you may cross double continuous white lines – can you give three instances?*
A. When turning right.
When passing an obstruction.
When told to do so by a policeman in uniform.

Q. *Can you cross a hazard warning line to overtake?*
A. Yes, provided it is safe to do so.

Parking, Waiting, Loading and Unloading

Q. *What signs or markings prohibit waiting and parking?*
A. No waiting sign; clearway sign; yellow lines in the gutter; double white line in the road.

Q. *What do three yellow stripes on the kerb edge mean?*
A. No loading or unloading during every working day and additional times.

Q. *What does a broken yellow line in the gutter mean?*
A. No waiting during any other period.

Q. *What do two yellow stripes on the kerb edge plus a single continuous yellow line along the gutter mean?*
A. No loading or unloading during every working day and no waiting during every working day.

Overtaking

Q. *When being overtaken, what must you not do?*
A. Do not increase your speed; in fact, slow down if it is necessary.

Q. *Can you give three examples where a driver must not overtake, because he cannot see far enough ahead?*
A. A corner or bend.
A hump back bridge.
A brow of a hill.

Q. *Other than those already mentioned, can you give a further six places where a driver should not overtake?*
A. 1. Where there is a 'no overtaking' sign being displayed.

2. Within the zig-zag area of a pedestrian crossing on the approach side.
3. At a road junction or crossroad.
4. At a level crossing.
5. Approaching any type of pedestrian crossing.
6. Where it would cause any other vehicle to swerve or slow down.

Q. *If you are driving alongside an operational bus lane when the vehicle in front stops to turn right, are you allowed to move into the bus lane (just for a moment) in order to overtake?*
A. No.

Headlights

Q. *What is the flashing of headlights used for?*
A. To let other road users know you are there.

Q. *Where and why would you not use full headlights?*
A. When travelling behind another vehicle – they may dazzle the driver via his mirror.
When negotiating a hump bridge – the headlights would shine into the sky.
When stationary – it is illegal.
In the face of oncoming traffic – they may dazzle.

Breakdowns and Accidents

Q. *If your vehicle breaks down by the side of the road, what should be the first thing to do?*
A. Warn traffic behind, ie hazard warning lights – red reflective triangle. Remember, at night do not let anyone obstruct your rear lights.

Q. *How far back should you place the reflective warning triangle?*
A. 50 metres (150 metres on the hard shoulder of motorways).

Q. *If anything falls from your vehicle on an ordinary road, what should you do?*
A. Stop as soon as you can do so safely and remove it from the carriageway.

Q. *If you are first on the scene of a road accident, what should you do?*
A. 1. Warn other traffic.
2. Eliminate any fire risk.
3. Arrange for police or ambulance.
4. Give first aid where necessary.
5. Stay at the scene until emergency services arrive.

Q. *If the accident involves a vehicle carrying dangerous goods, what else should be done?*
A. Arrange for the police or fire brigade as soon as possible – keep everyone away.
Keep well clear of any dust or vapour.

Q. *Give three occasions when the horn must not be used.*
A. Between 23.30 and 07.00 hours (11.30 pm and 7.00 am) in built-up areas.
   When the vehicle is stationary, except in an emergency.
   As a rebuke.

Blind Spots

Q. *When must the blind spot be checked?*
A. Prior to moving off.
   Prior to opening the door.
   Prior to reversing.

Drinking and Driving

Q. *What are the general rules regarding drinking and driving?*
A. Do not drink and drive.

Q. *What is the maximum permitted level of alcohol?*
A. 35 microgrammes of alcohol per 100 millilitres of breath.

Q. *How can alcohol affect your driving?*
A. It reduces co-ordination.
   It increases reaction time.
   It impairs judgement of speed and distance.

Q. *What are the penalties for driving while above the legal limit?*
A. Disqualification.
   Heavy fine.
   Imprisonment.

General

Q. *If your vehicle is fitted with a hand held telephone when must you not use it?*
A. When the vehicle is moving, except in an emergency.
   You must not stop on the hard shoulder of a motorway to answer or make a call however urgent.

Q. *Driving for long distances may make you feel sleepy. What can be done to prevent this happening?*
A. Make sure there is plenty of ventilation and fresh air in your vehicle.
   Stop at a suitable parking place and rest.

Q. *What should you do if you are driving along when you hear two-tone horns or sirens?*
A. Move over and make way for ambulance, fire or police vehicles.

Chapter 11
Vehicle Safety Questions

Each of the following questions is designed to assist the driver when answering questions put by driving examiners. They will help to give a more comprehensive knowledge of the workings of the vehicle.

Vehicle Checks

Q. *What mechanical and legal checks should you make on a Large Goods Vehicle before commencing a journey?*
A. Oil, fuel, coolant, windows, lights, road fund licence, operator's licence, air guage, tyres, mirrors, audible warning devices.

Q. *When is the best time to check the oil?*
A. After the vehicle has been standing for some time and the oil has had time to settle, ie first thing in the morning before starting the engine.

Brakes

Q. *What low pressure warning devices are fitted to vehicles?*
A. Gauge, buzzer, light.

Q. *What action would you take if your low pressure warning device started to operate while the vehicle was in motion?*
A. Stop, park safely until trouble is rectified.

Q. *In the hydraulic braking system, what does the necessity for pumping the pedal indicate?*
A. Shoes out of adjustment or air in the system.

Q. *What is meant by reserve travel?*
A. The distance left on the brake quadrant when the hand brake is in the 'on' position.

Q. *Why does the vehicle dip forward when the brakes are applied?*
A. Weight transfer causes more weight to be applied to the front springs and less to the rear.

Q. *How do air brakes work?*

A. Air is compressed by an engine-driven compressor and fed to one or more storage tanks. When the brake pedal is depressed a valve opens, permitting the compressed air to move pistons mounted near the wheels which operate the brake shoes.

Q. *What is a simple test for locating leaks in the air brake system?*

A. With pressure built up, get someone to depress the brake pedal. The position of the leak will then be heard as a loud hiss.

Q. *With air brakes, why is it dangerous to coast downhill?*

A. Air pressure may not build up when the engine is just ticking over, particularly with a worn compressor.

Q. *What is meant by brake fade?*

A. The frictional characteristics of the lining are affected by heat, the brake drums get hot and expand from the shoes, resulting in reduced braking efficiency, especially on long down gradients when the brakes have been excessively used and have become very hot.

Q. *How often should the air tanks of an air brake vehicle be drained?*

A. Daily.

Q. *With air brake vehicles, what is the safe minimum reading on the pressure gauge?*

A. 50–60 lb/sq in or the equivalent BAR reading.

Q. *In frosty weather, what could prevent air pressure building up in the brake reservoir?*

A. Moisture in the air drawn in by the compressor freezing in the brake system.

Q. *How can you prevent the moisture in the air brake system from building up?*

A. Drain the air tanks regularly – usually at the end of each working day.

Steering

Q. *What is meant by power assisted steering?*

A. A hydraulic system designed to relieve the driver of some of the effort required to turn the steering wheel against tyre friction and the weight on the steering axle.

Q. *If power assisted steering fails, how will this affect the control of the vehicle?*

A. Steering movements will be slow and heavy, and require much more effort by the driver.

Tyres

Q. *What is the legal requirement with regard to tyre safety?*
A. Correct pressure. Tread depth of no less than 1 mm. No breaks or cuts in the fabric in excess of 2.54 cm or 10% of the section width of tyre, whichever is the greater. No part of ply or cord to be exposed.

Q. *If you had a brick trapped between twin tyres, how would you remove it?*
A. First, try to prise it out; if this fails, jack up the offending wheel, slacken off the wheel nuts and then remove the brick.

Q. *What will cause a tyre to wear only on the shoulders?*
A. Underinflation.

Q. *What will cause a tyre to wear only on the middle?*
A. Over-inflation.

Windscreens

Q. *What types of glass are used in windscreens?*
A. Toughened and laminated.

Q. *How would toughened glass differ from laminated glass in the event of a broken windscreen?*
A. Vision is seriously reduced when toughened glass breaks; this does not happen with laminated.

Q. *If your toughened windscreen is broken, what action should be taken before moving the vehicle?*
A. Knock out the glass in order to obtain clear vision.

Q. *Is it an offence to drive a vehicle with a dirty windscreen?*
A. Yes.

Q. *Is it an offence to drive a vehicle with the windscreen washer bottle empty?*
A. Yes.

Two-speed Axles

Q. *What is a two-speed axle?*
A. An alternative reduction gear fitted to the back axle which doubles the number of available gear ratios.

Safe Loading

Q. *What safety factors are involved in the loading of a vehicle?*
A. To prevent load or any part of it endangering other road users. To ensure maximum stability and road holding when cornering or braking. To prevent any movement of the load if sudden braking is necessary.

Q. *If you were using two sheets to sheet a load, which sheet would you put on first?*

A. The rear sheet first, so that the front sheet will overlap the rear sheet; this will prevent the wind from getting under the sheet when the vehicle is being driven.

Vehicle faults

Q. *If excessive smoke comes from the vehicle's exhaust, what does this tell you and what should you do?*

A. The engine is faulty – you must stop your vehicle until rectified.

Q. *If your vehicle runs out of fuel and will not start after refuelling what should you do?*

A. A driver should never allow his vehicle to run out of fuel. However, if this situation does occur, he should bleed the fuel pump.

Lights

Q. *Drivers should always carry spare bulbs to replace any which may become unserviceable during the day – why?*

A. Because it is an offence not to have all lights clean and in working order.

Q. *When should you switch your lights on?*

A. At lighting up time.
On all roads at night where there is no street lighting.
On roads at night where the street lamps are less than 185 metres apart.
At any time of the day or night where visibility is impaired, eg poor light, heavy rain, fog or mist, falling snow.

Q. *When may a driver use his high intensity rear fog lamps?*

A. When visibility is seriously reduced to a distance of less than 100 metres.

Breakdown

Q. *If you break down by the side of the road, what must you do?*

A. First warn traffic behind (hazard warning lights, etc) and then diagnose the fault.

Q. *If you break down by the side of the road, how far back should you place the red reflector warning triangle?*

A. 50 metres on an ordinary road.
150 metres on the hard shoulder of a motorway.

Q. *If you break down by the side of the road, how far back should you place the warning traffic cones?*

A. The first cone should be placed about 15 metres from the obstruction and next to the kerb. The second cone should be in line with the outside of the vehicle but care should be taken not to obstruct rear lights and reflectors.

Chapter 12

True or False?

Only *one* of the answers shown after each of the following questions is correct. Check your answers against those given at the foot of each page.

(1) *When about to be overtaken a driver should:*
   A. 'Wave' the overtaking vehicle past.
   B. Sound the horn.
   C. Pull in to the left.
   D. Maintain a steady course.

(2) *The following classes of road user are NOT allowed on motorways:*
   A. Pedestrians.
   B. Motorcycles under 150cc.
   C. Vehicles with trailers.

(3) *A driver may overtake the vehicle in front on the left:*
   A. At no time.
   B. In a one-way street.
   C. On a dual carriageway.

(4) *On a three-lane motorway the outer (right hand) lane is for:*
   A. Fast moving traffic.
   B. Slow moving traffic.
   C. Overtaking only.

(5) *Where a pedestrian crossing is split by an island:*
   A. It should be treated as two crossings.
   B. It should still be treated as one crossing.
   C. It denotes a 40 mph speed limit.

Answers: (1)D (2)A (3)B (4)C (5)A

(6) *When crossing or turning right at a dual carriageway where the central reserve of the carriageway is too narrow for the length of the vehicle, drivers should:*
A. Wait until the road is clear from the right then proceed to the middle, then wait until the road is clear from the left.
B. Wait in the side road until both sides of the carriageway are clear enough for the driver to make the move in one continuous movement.
C. Treat each half separately and on its own merit.

(7) *What does the Highway Code advise 'If in doubt . . . '*
A. Slow down.
B. Hold back.
C. Do not overtake.

(8) *A junction with double broken white lines across its exit means:*
A. Stop at the junction.
B. Slow at the junction.
C. Give way at the junction.

(9) *When stopping a vehicle in an emergency:*
A. The brake and clutch should be depressed simultaneously.
B. The brake should be depressed before the clutch.
C. The brake should be depressed after the clutch.

(10) *If a roundabout is clear of other traffic, drivers:*
A. May take the most convenient route through the roundabout.
B. *Must* keep in your own lane through the roundabout.
C. *Must* keep to the left of the roundabout at all times.

(11) *If you are driving along single track road and the driver behind wants to pass but the first passing place you come to is on your right, you should:*
A. Drive on until you find a passing place on your own side.
B. Wait opposite the passing place and allow the other vehicle to pass you on your right.
C. Move over into the passing place and allow the other vehicle to pass you on your left.

(12) *When turning right out of a road wide enough for only one line of traffic in each direction, drivers should:*
A. Position just left of the centre of the road.
B. Position well to the left.
C. Position well to the right.

Answers: (6)B (7)C (8)C (9)B (10)A (11)B (12)B

(13) *It is an offence to leave a vehicle parked:*
    A. With the gear lever in neutral.
    B. With the doors open.
    C. With the headlights on.

(14) *On a winter night you run onto an ice-bound road. What is the first warning you get?*
    A. Your back end slides sideways.
    B. Your steering starts to feel light.
    C. Your wheels lock under braking.

(15) *If the back end of your articulated vehicle (the trailer) starts sliding to the right, the driver should:*
    A. Turn the steering wheel to the right.
    B. Turn the steering wheel to the left.
    C. Let go of the steering wheel and allow it to find its own correcting position.

(16) *Automatic warning signals on most motorways are:*
    A. Mounted overhead.
    B. At one-mile intervals.
    C. Mounted on the central reserve.

(17) *When in a slow moving 'traffic queue' situation drivers should ensure that:*
    A. The right-hand lane is used when overtaking.
    B. Zebra crossings are left clear.
    C. A vehicle-length gap is observed at all times.

(18) *On two-lane motorways, LGVs towing trailers:*
    A. Must not use the second (outer) lane.
    B. May use the second lane for overtaking only.
    C. Must not use them at all.

(19) *When entering or leaving property bordering on a road, drivers should:*
    A. Give way to vehicles from the immediate right.
    B. Give way to pedestrians as well as to traffic on the road.
    C. Stop.

(20) *Which is the safest gap to allow between your vehicle and the one you are following:*
    A. Your thinking distance.
    B. Your braking distance.
    C. Your overall stopping distance.

Answers: (13)C (14)B (15)A (16)C (17)B (18)B (19)B (20)C

(21) *The Highway Code specifically advises the driver to obtain the assistance of a guide when reversing:*
    A. From a side road.
    B. Into a narrow door or opening.
    C. If he cannot see clearly behind.

(22) *When you leave a motorway, you are required to alter your driving to suit the different conditions on other roads. In order to assist you in this, the Highway Code advises that you should be sure to use:*
    A. Your mirrors.
    B. Your speedometer.
    C. Your brakes and gears.

(23) *In a convex mirror – as against a flat one – following vehicles seem to be:*
    A. Nearer.
    B. Further away.
    C. Moving faster.

(24) *The maximum speed limit for a Class 1 38 tonnes LGV on a two-lane motorway is:*
    A. 50 mph.
    B. 60 mph.
    C. 40 mph.

(25) *A single broken white line with long markings and short gaps is:*
    A. A hazard warning line.
    B. A centre line.
    C. A lane line.

(26) *When the flashing amber light goes out at a pelican crossing, the next light to come on will be:*
    A. Green.
    B. Red.
    C. Steady amber.

(27) *If you break down on a motorway, you must:*
    A. Leave the motorway at the first exit.
    B. Get the vehicle on to the slip road.
    C. Get the vehicle on to the hard shoulder.

(28) *On narrow or winding roads or where there is a lot of oncoming traffic, drivers of large or slow moving vehicles should:*
    A. Be prepared to slow down or stop to allow faster traffic to overtake.
    B. Make every effort to drive as fast as possible so as not to slow down other faster traffic.
    C. Wave on traffic behind when it appears safe for them to overtake.

Answers: (21)C (22)B (23)B (24)B (25)A (26)A (27)C (28)A

(29) *Drivers should never stop on or immediately beyond a:*
   A. Box junction.
   B. Roundabout.
   C. Level crossing.

(30) *Travelling on an empty motorway at 60 mph, which lane should you use?*
   A. The first lane (nearside).
   B. The second lane (middle).
   C. The third lane (offside).

Answers: (29)C (30)A

Chapter 13
Youth Training for the Transport Industry (National Vocational Qualification – NVQ)

Under the auspices of government training, various training schemes have been introduced.

Some of these courses have been designed with road transport in mind and most certainly open the door to the transport industry for young people who would otherwise never have the opportunity of entering the industry.

These transport courses involve intensive training at a selected transport training group or equivalent body supported by real work experience – supplementary training at a selected transport company.

These high level transport training courses offer off-the-job training which can include some or all of the following:

(a) Life skills in transport
(b) Light vehicle 'driver' training
(c) Fork-lift truck operation
(d) First aid
(e) Associated knowledge for young drivers
(f) Safety procedures in transport
(g) Workshop practice
(h) Warehouse and distribution theory
(i) Road Transport Regulations

These courses can offer a number of professionally recognised qualifications, certificates and licences:

(a) Fork Lift Truck Operators Certificate
(b) Driving Licence   leading to a full
(c) Driving Test (Pass Certificate)   driving licence
(d) First Aid Certificate
(e) National Vocational Qualification (NVQ) at Levels 1 and 2 in Wholesale and Warehousing

Fork-Lift Truck Operation

It is a requirement that all fork-lift truck (FLT) operators have been properly trained or have taken a formal course of FLT instruction and have been tested and awarded a FLT Certificate of Competence.

Most road transport courses include FLT training which takes the trainee step-by-step through the basic FLT operation. Normal FLT courses are of one week's duration and involve truck maintenance, practical and theoretical training. On completion of this training the trainee will be subjected to a written practical and oral test. Successful trainees will be awarded a certificate of competence for the appropriate truck – counter balance or reach. The minimum age requirement for this training is 17 years.

Driving Test and Licence

On reaching the age of 17 trainees will require a provisional licence, after which a full course of driver training will follow. It is usual for this training to be condensed into two working weeks of intensive behind-the-wheel light vehicle driver training. At the end of this period the trainee will go forward to take the statutory driving test.

It is usual on this type of course for the trainee to be given some form of instruction on a larger vehicle such as a transit or its equivalent, giving the trainee a little experience of driving small goods vehicles.

First Aid Certification Course

Because of the nature of the job done within the road transport industry it is good sense to have a First Aid course included. These courses are usually run by or in conjunction with St John's Ambulance and the British Red Cross. They are usually one week Certification Courses where the course member is taught and at the end of the course is tested both practically and verbally. Successful trainees will be awarded either First Aid Essentials Certificate or the First Aid at Work Certificate or its equivalent.

On The Job Training

On-the-job training will take place at a selected transport company where the trainee will be taken step-by-step through all aspects of the transport operation, from warehouse and yard duties to working in the transport office.

The course curriculum varies slightly to suit the needs and demands of the different types of transport operation, but the practical experience offered is usually the same and may include:

Driver's Mate
Helping the driver to load and unload his vehicle, delivering goods and

cargoes, route planning and reading maps, keeping records and completing tachograph charts, developing communication skills and customer relations.

Working in the Traffic Office
Booking goods in and out, routing and scheduling, reading and checking tachograph charts, dealing with drivers and customers, use of various office equipment, developing initiative and enterprise.

Warehouse and Yard Duties
Fork-lift driving, kinetic handling, loading pallets, loading and unloading vehicles, roping and sheeting, blocking and stacking goods. Also, checking the condition and correct number of goods being loaded or unloaded, taking the appropriate action in the case of shortage or damaged goods and stacking or storing safely.

Working in the Garage
Helping the vehicle mechanic or fitter to service and repair company vehicles, use of various work shop equipment, use of hand tools, and numerous other work shop duties.

Candidates wishing to know more about these courses should contact their local Careers Office, Job Centre or Training Group. Trainees will normally be required to take part in a pre-entry selection test. Subject to the result of this test the trainee will be invited for an interview for the course organisers to assess the suitability of the applicant for this particular type of course.

Note: Just one word of warning – these *Introduction to Road Transport and Distribution Courses* are without doubt the best transport courses ever run for young people but ONLY those who REALLY want to work in the transport industry should apply. A lot of young people are attracted to this type of course because they like the idea of learning to drive, but the driving part of the course is nearly always left to the end because of the age restrictions, ie candidates must be 17 years of age to hold a Group A ordinary driving licence.

A trainee's wage allowance under the two-year youth training is currently £29.50 per week, or £35.00 per week subject to age, plus travelling expenses over the first £3.00.

These allowances are constantly under review and may be increased or may be subsidised by workplace Providers.

Wholesale and Warehouse National Vocational Qualification

The *Training and Enterprise Council (TEC)* are sponsoring In-company training and assessments in the field of Wholesale and Warehousing.

Through the medium of the local TEC initiative Managing Agents are able to offer a full training package for individuals aged between 16 and 18 and possibly between 19 and 25 years.

Training is competence based and takes place in the workplace doing the job to National Standards and is assessed in the workplace by qualified Assessors.

A training Log and Assessment Record are provided to each individual identifying tasks and competences common to the Wholesale and Warehouse Industry. Achievement of these competences by an individual is recognised by the Industry Lead Body and provides evidence for the Wholesale and Warehouse National Vocational Qualification at Level 1 and 2.

This National Qualification is awarded jointly by The National Wholesale Training Council and The City and Guild London Institute. Individuals who have successfully completed Levels 1 and 2 of this Training Programme and have reached the age of 17 years or over will qualify for further training as Fork Lift Truck Operators, with an added bonus of a driving course.

Further information is available from your local Training and Enterprise Council.

Commercial LGV Driver Training Centres and Group Training Associations

England

Avon

Severn Transport Training Ltd,
7 Upper Perry Hill,
Southville,
Bristol BS3 1NH

Western Driver Training Services,
c/o Western Transport Ltd,
Severn Side Trading Estate,
St Andrews Road,
Avonmouth BS11 8AG

Bedfordshire

Commercial Transport Training,
c/o TWF Ltd,
Stanbridge Road,
Leighton Buzzard LU7 8QH

Berkshire

PVZ Systems Ltd,
t/a Big Wheelers,
1A Randolph Road,
Reading RG1 8EB

Fullers Transport Ltd,
475 Malton Avenue Trading Estate,
Slough SL1 4QU

Cambridgeshire

B Collins,
Littleport Driving School,
Black Horse Drive,
Littleport,
Ely CB6 1EG

Mid Anglia Training Ltd,
138 Peterborough Road,
Whittlesey,
Peterborough PE17 1PD

National Carriers Ltd,
Bourges Boulevard,
Peterborough

Cheshire

Runcorn Transport Services Ltd,
Picow Farm Road,
Runcorn,
Cheshire WA7 4UW

North Cheshire Training
Association Ltd,
Unit 11/4,
Palatine Industrial Estate,
Causeway Avenue,
off Wilderspool Causeway,
Warrington WA4 6QQ

Warrington HGV Training,
Navigation Street,
Howley Lane,
Warrington WA1 2DW

Cleveland

Teesside Transport Training
Association Ltd,
Hamilton House,
Cargo Fleet Lane,
Middlesbrough TS3 8DG

Cornwall

Cornwall Transport Training Ltd,
Trenowah Road,
Holmbush,
St Austell PL25 3EB

Cumbria

Training Services (Carlisle) Ltd,
Road Transport Training Centre,
Parkhill Road,
Kingstown Industrial Estate,
Kingstown,
Carlisle CA3 0EX

Derbyshire

Tarmac Heavy Vehicles Driving
School,
Cawdor Quarry,
Matlock

Devon

Devon Transport Training Ltd,
Lion Rest Estate,
Station Road,
Exminster,
Nr Exeter EX6 8DZ

South Devon Training Group Ltd,
8 Fairfax Road,
Heathfield,
Newton Abbot TQ12 6UD

Dorset

Wessex Transport Training Ltd,
ITEC House,
West Quay Road,
Poole BH15 1LA

Durham

Darlington DTS Ltd,
Interfreight House,
Whessoe Road,
Darlington,
Co Durham DL3 0XE

Essex

TDT Management Services Ltd,
London Road,
Kelvedon,
Colchester CO5 9AU

Havering & District Training
Services Ltd,
Manor House,
River Way,
Harlow CM20 2EZ

Basildon & District Transport and
Industrial Training Ltd,
210 Cumberland Avenue,
South Benfleet S57 1DY

Silcock Express,
Beam Park,
off Thames Avenue,
Dagenham

Gloucestershire

R C Oldmeadow,
t/a Gloucestershire Transport
Training Services,
Staverton Airport,
Churchdown GL51 6SP

Three Counties Training Services,
Monk Meadow Training Estate,
Hempstead Lane,
Gloucester

Greater Manchester

Manchester Training Group,
Greengate,
Middleton M24 1RU

Hampshire

Portsmouth & District Transport
Training Ltd,
Old Goods Yard (Upside),
Fareham Station,
Fareham PO14 1AA

Herefordshire

Three Counties Training Services,
12 Cattle Market,
Hereford HR4 9HX

Hertfordshire

West Herts Transport Training Ltd,
VER House,
Park Industrial Estate,
Frogmore,
St Albans AL2 2DR

National Carriers Ltd,
Balmoral Road,
Watford

Humberside

Management & Industrial Training
Services Ltd,
260 Macaulay Street,
Grimsby DN31 2EY

Training for Industry Ltd,
Willow House,
Clay Street,
Chamberlain Road,
Hull HU8 8HA

Kent

Kent and Sussex Training Services,
London Road,
Dunkirk,
Nr Faversham ME13 9LG

Carlton Motor School,
145 Canterbury Street,
Gillingham ME7 5TT

Kentish Bus and Coach Co Ltd,
Central Road,
Dartford D91 5BG

BOC Transhield Ltd,
Oare Road,
Faversham

Gordon Springate Transport
Training Services,
County Showground,
Detling,
Maidstone MEL4 3JF

Lancashire

North Lancashire Road Haulage
Training School,
Transport House,
Whalley Road,
Altham West,
Accrington BB5 1DS

Lancaster Training Services Ltd,
The Training Centre,
St George's Quay,
Lancaster LA1 5QJ

Leicestershire

Driver Training & Management
Services Ltd,
West Street,
Earl Shilton LE9 7EJ

Garage & Transport Training (South
Leicestershire) Ltd,
Rossendale Road,
Earl Shilton LE9 7LX

J Coates (HGV Services) Ltd,
45–50 Great Central Street,
Leicester

London (postal districts)

Road Transport Associates of
London Limited,
Catford Stadium Car Park,
Adenmore Road, Catford,
London SE6 4RJ

Henderson Transport Training
Services,
The Portacabin,
Wimbledon Stadium Car Park,
Plough Lane,
London SW17

115

Merseyside

Knowsley Transport Training Ltd,
Stockpit Lane,
Knowsley Industrial Park,
Kirkby,
Liverpool L33 7SE

Sutton and Sons (St Helens) Ltd,
Sutton Heath,
St Helens,
WA9 5BW

Middlesex

Extra Staff HGV,
16 London Road,
Staines TW18 4BP

Norfolk

Transport Training (Norfolk) Ltd,
Harford Centre,
Hall Road,
Norwich NR4 6DE

Thetford Transport Training,
2 Redgate,
Thetford IP24 2HA

Northamptonshire

Northants Road Transport
Training Ltd,
Stour Road,
Weedon Road Industrial Estate,
Northampton NN5 5AA

Nottinghamshire

A R Marshall & Sons (Bulwell) Ltd,
Forest House,
Hucknall Lane,
Bulwell,
Nottingham

Trent Transport Training Ltd,
Artic Way,
Kimberley NG16 2HS

North Nottinghamshire Haulage
GTA,
Claylands Avenue,
Worksop S81 7DJ

Oxfordshire

Thames Valley Training,
Milton Trading Estate,
Milton,
Abingdon OX14 4RZ

Hinton and Higgs Transport and
Training,
20 Marcham Road
Abingdon OX14 1AA

Rollright School of Transport Ltd,
Enstone Airfield Complex,
Enstone,
Oxford OX7 4NN

Shropshire

Mike Bowler Shropshire Transport
Training,
Rednel Industrial Estate,
Queens Head,
Oswestry

Somerset

Somerset Training Services Ltd,
Bristol Road,
Dunball,
Bridgwater TA6 4TF

South Yorkshire

South Yorkshire Hauliers Training
Group Ltd,
Shepcote Training Centre,
Shepcote Lane,
Sheffield S9 1US

Staffordshire

Leek & Norton School of Motoring,
Broad Street,
Leek

Bassett Group of Companies,
Transport House,
Tittensor,
Stoke-on-Trent

Suffolk

RTT Training Services Ltd,
The Old Airfield,
Norwich Road,
Mendlesham,
Stowmarket IP14 5ND

Surrey

EP Training Services Ltd,
6A High Street,
Esher KT10 9RT

Cory Distribution Ltd,
190 London Road,
Hackbridge SM6 7EB

Sussex

Millers Transport Training,
Goodwood Motor Circuit,
Chichester,
West Sussex PO78 0PH

South Coast HGV Driver Training,
Sidley Goods Yard,
Ninfield Road,
Sidley,
Bexhill-on-Sea,
East Sussex

Tyne and Wear

Tyneside TS Ltd,
Airport Industrial Estate,
Kingston Park,
Kenton,
Newcastle-upon-Tyne NE3 2EF

Warwickshire

Heart of England Transport
Training Services,
Curriers Close,
Canley,
Coventry CV4 8AW

Warwickshire County Council,
PO Box 50,
Shire Hall,
Warwick CV34 4RJ

West Midlands

Birmingham Training Services,
Granby Avenue,
Garretts Green Industrial Estate,
Garretts Green,
Birmingham

Midlands BRS Ltd,
Driver Training Centre,
Bromford Lane,
Birmingham B24 8DP

SPD Group Ltd,
Wellington Road,
Perry Road,
Birmingham

West Midlands Training Group Ltd,
Dudley Road,
Kingswinford DY6 8BS

S Jones Industrial Holdings Ltd,
Anglian Road,
Aldridge,
Walsall WS9 8ET

West Yorkshire

Liquids, Powders & Gas Transport
Co Ltd,
Nab Lane,
Birstall,
Batley

Onward Transport Ltd,
Wakefield Road,
Ackworth,
Pontefract WF7 7BE

Bradford and District Hauliers GTA
Ltd,
420 Tong Street,
Bradford BD4 6LP

Leeds TT Group Ltd,
24 Ashfield Way,
Whitehall Estate,
Whitehall Road,
Leeds LS12 5JB

National Carriers Ltd,
Marsh Lane,
Leeds

Ackworth Transport Ltd,
Wakefield Road,
Ackworth,
Pontefract

Wiltshire

Wiltshire Transport Training Ltd,
Hopton Industrial Estate,
London Road,
Devizes SN10 2EX

Scotland

Central

Safe Group Training Limited,
Seabegs Road,
Bonnybridge FK4 2AQ

Fife

Fife Transport Training Centre Ltd,
Randolph Place,
Kirkaldy KY1 2YX

Grampian

John Gilbert Transport Training,
Cloverhill Road,
Bridge of Don,
Aberdeen

Highland

Moray Firth GTA,
32 Harbour Road,
Inverness IV1 1SY

Lothian

South of Scotland Group Training
(Edinburgh) Ltd,
Loanhead Road,
Straiton EH20 9NQ

Strathclyde

LAGTA Ltd,
7 Palacecraig Street,
Shawhead,
Coatbridge ML5 4TS

Glasgow Road Haulage GTA Ltd,
120 Crowhill Road,
Bishopbriggs,
Glasgow

W H Malcolm Ltd,
Murray Street,
Paisley PA3 1QQ

Tayside

Tayside Road Transport GTA Ltd,
Smeaton Road,
Wester Gourdie,
Dundee DD1 4UT

Wales

Clwyd

West Cheshire Training Association
Ltd,
Building 243/E5,
Deeside Industrial Estate,
Queensferry CM5 2LR

Gatewen Transport Training Ltd,
Gatewen,
New Broughton,
Wrexham LL11 6YA

Gwent

Heads of the Valley Transport
GTA Ltd,
Ty mawr Road,
Gilwern NP7 0EB

Mid Glamorgan

Western Brothers Ltd,
Waterton Road,
Bridgend CF31 3YS

R C Hutchings,
t/a UK (Commercial Driving
School),
216 Corporation Road,
Newport

Powys

Abermule Transport Training,
Station Yard,
Kerry Road,
Abermule,
Newtown

South Glamorgan

Cardiff and Newport RH Training
Association Ltd,
St Albany Road,
Fleetway,
Cardiff CF1 7UH

West Glamorgan

Swansea Road Transport Training
Ltd,
Training Centre,
New Industrial Estate,
Off Nantyffin Road,
Llansamlet,
Swansea SA7 9ED

Henderson Transport Training
Services,
The Portacabin,
Wimbledon Stadium Car Park,
Plough Lane,
London SW17

Merseyside

Knowsley Transport Training Ltd,
Stockpit Lane,
Knowsley Industrial Park,
Kirkby,
Liverpool L33 7SE

Sutton and Sons (St Helens) Ltd,
Sutton Heath,
St Helens,
WA9 5BW

Middlesex

Extra Staff HGV,
16 London Road,
Staines TW18 4BP

Norfolk

Transport Training (Norfolk) Ltd,
Harford Centre,
Hall Road,
Norwich NR4 6DE

Thetford Transport Training,
2 Redgate,
Thetford IP24 2HA

Northamptonshire

Northants Road Transport
Training Ltd,
Stour Road,
Weedon Road Industrial Estate,
Northampton NN5 5AA

Nottinghamshire

A R Marshall & Sons (Bulwell) Ltd,
Forest House,
Hucknall Lane,
Bulwell,
Nottingham

Trent Transport Training Ltd,
Artic Way,
Kimberley NG16 2HS

North Nottinghamshire Haulage
GTA,
Claylands Avenue,
Worksop S81 7DJ

Oxfordshire

Thames Valley Training,
Milton Trading Estate,
Milton,
Abingdon OX14 4RZ

Hinton and Higgs Transport and
Training,
20 Marcham Road
Abingdon OX14 1AA

Rollright School of Transport Ltd,
Enstone Airfield Complex,
Enstone,
Oxford OX7 4NN

Shropshire

Mike Bowler Shropshire Transport
Training,
Rednel Industrial Estate,
Queens Head,
Oswestry

Somerset

Somerset Training Services Ltd,
Bristol Road,
Dunball,
Bridgwater TA6 4TF

South Yorkshire

South Yorkshire Hauliers Training
Group Ltd,
Shepcote Training Centre,
Shepcote Lane,
Sheffield S9 1US

Traffic Area Offices

North Western

Portcullis House,
Seymour Grove,
Manchester M16 0NE
Tel 061-872 5077

the Metropolitan Counties of Greater Manchester and Merseyside, the Counties of Cheshire, Clwyd, Cumbria, Gwynedd and Lancashire, the Borough of High Peak, in the County of Derbyshire.

North Eastern

Westgate House,
Westgate Road,
Newcastle-upon-Tyne NE1 1TW
Tel 091-261 0031
and
Hillcrest House,
386 Harehills Lane,
Leeds LS9 6NF
Tel 0532 499433

the Metropolitan Counties of South Yorkshire, Tyne and Wear and West Yorkshire, the Counties of Cleveland, Durham, Humberside, Northumberland and North Yorkshire

West Midland

Cumberland House,
200 Broad Street,
Birmingham B15 1TD
Tel 021-631 3300

the Metropolitan County of West Midlands, the Counties of Hereford and Worcester, Shropshire, Staffordshire and Warwickshire.

Eastern

Terrington House,
13–15 Hills Road,
Cambridge CB2 1NP
Tel 0223 358922
and
Birbeck House,
14–16 Trinity Square,
Nottingham NG1 4BA
Tel 0602 475511

the Counties of Bedfordshire, Cambridgeshire, Leicestershire, Lincolnshire, Norfolk, Northamptonshire, Nottinghamshire and Suffolk, the County of Derbyshire except the Borough of High Peak, the County of Essex except the Districts of Basildon, Brentwood, Epping Forest and Harlow and the the Borough of Thurrock.

South Wales

Caradog House,
1–6 St Andrews Place,
Cardiff CF1 3PW
Tel 0222 394027

*the Counties of Dyfed, Gwent,
Mid Glamorgan, Powys, South
Glamorgan and West Glamorgan.*

Western

The Gaunts' House,
Denmark Street,
Bristol BS1 5DR
Tel 0272 297221

*the Counties of Avon, Cornwall,
Devon, Dorset, Gloucestershire,
Somerset and Wiltshire.*

Metropolitan

Charles House,
357 Kensington High Street,
London W14 8QH
Tel 071-605 0347

*the administrative area of Greater
London, the County of Hertfordshire,
the County of Surrey except the
Borough of Surrey Heath and the
district of Waverley, the districts of
Basildon, Brentwood, Epping Forest
and Harlow and the Borough of
Thurrock in the County of Essex, the
Borough of Dartford and the District of
Sevenoaks in the County of Kent.*

South Eastern

Ivy House,
3 Ivy Terrace,
Eastbourne BN21 4QT
Tel 0323 21471

*the Counties of Berkshire,
Buckinghamshire, East Sussex,
Hampshire, Isle of Wight, Oxfordshire
and West Sussex, the County of Kent
except the Borough of Dartford and the
District of Sevenoaks, the Borough of
Surrey Heath and the District of
Waverley in the County of Surrey.*

Scottish

83 Princes Street,
Edinburgh EH2 2ER
Tel 031-225 1880

Scotland

Conversion Table

Weights and Measures
1 yard = 0.9144 metres
1 mile = 1760 yards = 1.609 kilometres
1 square inch = 6.45 square centimetres
1 cubic foot = 1728 cubic inches = 0.0283 cubic metres
1 pint = 20 fluid ounces = 34.68 cubic inches = 0.568 litres
1 gallon = 4.546 litres
1 ounce = 28.35 grams
1 pound = 16 ounces = 0.4536 kilograms
1 hundredweight = 50.80 kilograms
1 ton = 20 hundredweight = 1.016 tonnes
1 metre = 1.094 yards
1 kilometre = 0.6214 miles
1 square metre = 1.196 square yards
1 cubic metre = 1.308 cubic yards
1 litre = 1.76 pints
1 kilogram = 2.205 pounds
1 tonne = 0.984 tons